Coumara
It's very
what Cisco
in the world of
solutions. IOT

MTConnect: will be
To Measure Is To Know huge
for cisco.

Hope

How and Why a Royalty-Free and Open-Source you
Standard Is Revolutionizing the you
Business and Technology of Manufacturing Enjoy

---

my
Book.

By
Dave Edstrom
CEO/CTO
Virtual Photons Electrons   Dave

Copyright © 2013

ISBN 978-0-9890742-0-9

Cover design by Suzanne Leonard and Dave Edstrom
Set in 12pt Cambria.

Published by Virtual Photons Electrons, LLC, in Ashburn, VA.

Printed and bound by Walls Lithographics in Chantilly, Virginia.

Table of Contents

Dedication

This book is dedicated to my wife of almost 30 years, Julie Hall Johnson Edstrom. The best thing that ever happened to me was when I met her at a party in West Springfield on Saturday December 15, 1979. I could write a book about how great she is, but I will save that book for another day. Julie helped edit this book and made great suggestions from day one.

I also dedicate this book to my parents, John and Ruth Edstrom, as they tell me all the time, without them, I would not be here. I affectionately call my parents Slim and Weasie. The Slim came from working at Wakefield Park one summer, where everyone in the basketball gym called everyone else Slim. It stuck permanently on my father. I call my mother Weasie because one day we were watching *The Jeffersons* (the TV show for you youngsters), and I said to my mom, "You sound just like Weasie on *The Jeffersons.*" It stuck. My parents grew up on farms and they truly know what hard work is all about. My mother was salutatorian in her class in Randolph, Minnesota, and she is a well-known professional artist, a seamstress, and an excellent golfer. My mother worked for the famous Dr. Rudolph Hermann and knew Dr. Wernher von Braun as well. Hermann and von Braun are legends, and von Braun is known as the "father of the American space program." My father was moved from 2nd grade to 4th grade because he was so smart, and he was captain of the football team, co-captain of the basketball team, and captain of the baseball team as well. He starred at St. Olaf when they won the 1953 national championship in football. The St. Olaf football team went undefeated in the Midwest Conference of the National Intercollegiate Athletic Association. They now compete in NCAA Division III. That team played both ways, i.e., offense and defense. The squad scored 362 points (tops in the country), shut out four opponents, and outgained the opposition 3,239 yards to 1,252. As the oldest of five kids he also had to help with all the chores on a 260-acre farm. The town minister had to convince my grandfather that my father should go to college. My father graduated from St. Olaf, became a pilot and air traffic controller in the United States Air Force, served two tours of duty in Vietnam, and is the world record holder for chronic lymphocytic leukemia (CLL). He got CLL while in Vietnam from agent orange. He is also an excellent golfer. I could not have asked for better parents.

I also dedicate this book to John, Michael, and Tim for being such great sons. A very special thanks to my son Michael for his editing suggestions as well. My three sons never gave my wife and me any problems, and I could not be more proud of them. Besides being great guys, excellent students (all three were in the National Honor Society) and fine athletes—all three could dunk on a 10-foot basketball goal by their 18th birthdays.

Last, but certainly not least, I dedicate this book to my sister—Dr. Julie Lynn Edstrom. She was the best athlete between the two of us and not by a little bit. She was an all-everything catcher in high school and starred at the college level as well. She coached softball at the high school and college level. She has a bachelor's, two master's, and her Ph.D. She is a high school counselor and runs her own counseling company. She has done an amazing job counseling kids and adults and helping those who are truly hurting in life. What she has accomplished will outweigh anything I will ever do in life—which is absolutely true and I could not be more proud of her.

I thank the numerous individuals who helped me understand and appreciate technology and the many people who have helped drive MTConnect later in this book in the Acknowledgements.

Foreword

On September 14, 2006, I received an email from Dave Edstrom asking if I would be interested in giving a keynote at the Association for Manufacturing Technology's (AMT) Annual Meeting. I was intrigued on the technical and economic challenges he stated manufacturing was facing, as he quoted AMT as telling him: "We are looking for a moon shot. We need that type of challenge to redefine our industry. If we don't totally reinvent ourselves we are dead."

After speaking with AMT's leadership, I agreed to give it a try since it was important, interesting, and a difficult challenge. One reason was that the keynote would be given on October 28, leaving just six weeks to get up to speed on manufacturing and to come up with a good idea. One potential path was to imitate the success of the IT industry by embracing open standards that made it easier for IT equipment to interoperate.

What came out of all of this were two talks at AMT's Annual Members' Meeting. Dave gave a presentation titled "How the Internet's Participation Age Will Drive Dramatic Changes in the Machine Tool Industry," and I gave a keynote titled "Creating a Thriving Manufacturing Base in 21st Century America." This keynote proposed creating an open and royalty-free standard to easily get information from manufacturing equipment on the shop floor, such as machine tools, to applications to enable improved productivity.

Dave and the AMT leadership came to visit me on November 30, 2006, at the University of California, Berkeley, to discuss how to turn this vision into a reality. I recruited my Berkeley research colleagues Armando Fox, David Dornfeld, and Will Sobel to help turn this concept into a standard with a working software implementation. MTConnect was born in the fall of 2006 and was formally kicked off in 2007.

It was exciting to visit the International Manufacturing Technology Show (IMTS) in 2008 to see MTConnect working with several machines on the exhibit floor.

I am very glad to see that MTConnect continues to thrive and has become a true game changer for manufacturing. I enjoyed working with Dave on MTConnect and believe this book, *MTConnect: To Measure Is To Know*, is a great way to learn not only about MTConnect, but also to understand the important principles and lessons learned from open systems that Dave shares with the reader.

—Dave Patterson

David A. Patterson joined the faculty of the University of California, Berkeley, in 1977. He is holder of the E.H. and M.E. Pardee Chair of Computer Science and is a member of the National Academy of Engineering and the National Academy of Sciences.

Introduction

Writing a book on both technology and MTConnect is something that I have been thinking about for a while. I started working on a technology book in 2008. In the spring of 2010, I decided to have this book focus on both open systems and MTConnect. I have spent 35 years in the computer industry and a few years in manufacturing, so I have learned a few things along the way. I have learned many things thanks to all the smart folks who I have had the privilege of working with over the decades.

I love to write about technology and have written countless articles and blog posts over the years and god knows how many presentations on technology. I have a number of good friends at Sun Microsystems who have written books on a variety of topics who strongly encouraged me to write this book. I love writing about MTConnect because it is a topic I never get tired of talking about, but this book is not just about MTConnect. It is first a book about how to properly think about open systems and technology and, most importantly, how to apply that thinking in manufacturing followed by the specifics on MTConnect. This is *both* a business and a technical book.

If you read my blog, any of the articles I have written, videos I have done, or seen a presentation that I have given, you will see a recurring theme of open systems and how to think about as well as execute problem solving. Whenever I create anything, whether I am consulting for a company, writing an article, creating a video, or anything that I am creating, I am careful to always make sure I own the intellectual property. I typically license what I do back in perpetuity, and there would be a reciprocal license, but I still take great care to own what I create. I certainly believe deeply in open systems, but I also strongly believe in giving credit where credit is due. On countless occasions I have sent my presentations or articles I have written to those who ask. I ask that I get the appropriate credit. If I can help you get the word out on MTConnect, please do not hesitate to drop me a note, and I will be glad to share. The goal of this book is to educate readers on open systems, change thinking on the application of technology in manufacturing, and get the word out on MTConnect.

One of the best days of my life was when Dr. Dave Patterson of the University of California, Berkeley, agreed to work with me on a pair of back-to-back keynotes at the Association for Manufacturing Technology's (AMT) Lake Las Vegas Meeting in October 2006. Together, we laid the foundation for MTConnect.

Who should read this book? Everyone! What else would you expect an author to say? Seriously, anyone who wants to better understand the lessons of open systems, how to think about problem solving, learn about MTConnect from a business perspective, and understand the MTConnect standard and protocol should read this book. Those who would benefit from reading this book and learning about MTConnect include:

- Anyone who wants to understand the right way to think about technology and its business and technical implications
- Shop owners, plant managers, and anyone in manufacturing interested in improving productivity
- Industry thought leaders
- MTConnect® Institute participants
- Equipment suppliers
- Students
- Professors
- Software developers
- Distributors

- Integrated Software Vendors (ISVs)
- Integrators
- Consultants
- Anyone wanting to learn more about open systems, problem solving, and how to think about the application of technology
- Anyone wanting to learn more about MTConnect

Why Should You Care About MTConnect?

Let's take a look at these different categories of individuals and understand their real motivation for caring about MTConnect.

Why Should a Shop Owner or Plant Manager Care About MTConnect? They want to make more money by being more productive. It is plain and simple. You cannot manage what you cannot measure. If you cannot easily network your manufacturing equipment and get meaningful data then you are managing in the dark.

Why Should Manufacturing Equipment Providers Care About MTConnect? They like having more and not less customers and by taking care of their customers they will have more customers. Shop owners and plant managers absolutely hate this proprietary madness nightmare of trying to get manufacturing equipment networked, and they are demanding a universal plug-n-play protocol. Plus, this saves manufacturing equipment providers time and money because the answer to software connectivity is one word—MTConnect.

Why Should Software Application Developers Care About MTConnect? Because software application developers would rather innovate their software as opposed to writing hundreds of different adapters that do nothing but connect systems. Yes, that is how some companies make their money, but most software companies are innovators and not just adapter writers.

Why Should Machinists Care About MTConnect? You
want to make more money and be more productive. I look at
machinists the same way I look at neurosurgeons. A machinist
wants to know everything about what is going on with the
machine tool and the making of a part in the exact same way a
neurosurgeon wants to know everything going on with a
patient during an operation. Don't think blood pressure is
important during an operation or the strength of the pulse?
Then you must not think it is important to know what is really
going on inside that machine tool either when you are making
a part. Do you think a neurosurgeon gets his scalpel from a
parts bin with no idea how many hours that scalpel has been
used? Of course not, but do you as a machinist know the exact
number of hours on a cutting tool? Today's surgeons are using
robots to do surgeries with the surgeons commanding the
robot to make the incision and perform the very delicate tasks.
Do you think a surgeon would like to know if the task
commanded varies from the task executed? How about the
machinist? Does the machinist want to know as well? Of course
they do!

Only one to two percent of all shops monitor their shop
floor. Initially, when I surveyed shop floor monitoring
companies, they felt the number was in the four to five percent
range, but after careful review they said it was more like one to
two percent. By monitoring your shop floor, I do not mean
someone walking around with a clipboard looking up at the
stack lights, marking down the status, entering it into a
spreadsheet and then later emailing it to management. I mean
the ability to know what is happening on your shop or plant
floor anywhere and at any time. The next time you go in for a
surgery, tell the surgeon that you want to save money and not
monitor any of your vital signs. Drop me a note and let me
know what the surgeon tells you. Then why is it that 98 to 99
percent of all shops don't bother monitoring their shop floor?

Think of MTConnect as simply the Bluetooth® of manufacturing that makes it easy to get information off your manufacturing equipment. MTConnect is not an application, but it makes it very easy for applications to read data in a common and universal format. "Different Devices, Common Connection" is what we say about MTConnect.

It is important to know that MTConnect stands for "Manufacturing Technology Connect" and not "Machine Tool Connect" as so many people think. It is an important point because MTConnect is not just about connecting machine tools, but all manufacturing technology.

MTConnect™ is a registered trademark of AMT—The Association for Manufacturing Technology.

An important point to make is that I wrote this book as Dave Edstrom the CEO/CTO of Virtual Photons Electrons. That is what you see on the front of my book. Yes, I am president and chairman of the Board for the MTConnect Institute, but let's be 100 percent clear, this book is not from the MTConnect Institute. It was not approved or blessed by the MTConnect Institute and it was not paid for by the MTConnect Institute, because an individual does not need approval or the blessing of the MTConnect Institute to write a blog post, an article, create a video, or write a book about MTConnect. That's one of the many beautiful aspects of the open, royalty-free, and open-source standard called MTConnect. I wear multiple hats in my consulting company and one of them happens to be president and chairman of the Board for the MTConnect Institute, which I am very proud to serve. My company, Virtual Photons Electrons, is a MTConnect Technical Advisory Group Member. With that disclaimer out of the way, let's get back to technology and MTConnect!

"MTConnect will be more important in the 21st century for manufacturing than CNC was for manufacturing in the 20th century." That is not my opinion, but the opinion of John Byrd, former president of AMT. Let's jump in and find out why John Byrd is correct!

Chapter 1: Igniting Change

Standardizing Manufacturing

A classic adage regarding standards is "the great thing about standards is that there are so many of them." When I suggested to John Byrd that the need existed for a common, open, and royalty-free standard to connect manufacturing equipment to the network, I had no idea that the concept of standards really started with manufacturing. I researched this and was fascinated with the story of a tool builder named William Sellers of the Franklin Institute in 1864 that I had found in my January 2002 copy of *Wired Magazine*. The article was excellent and was written by James Surowiecki of *The New Yorker*.[1] I remember reading this article and thinking what a powerful story it was regarding standards. This is a story and a lesson that manufacturing needs to understand and apply again in many areas. The MTConnect community has heard this story a few times, but it is worth retelling.

Figure 1. *William Sellers*[2]

William Sellers was a tool builder who believed there was a big problem with screws. The problem was multifold. First, there were way too many types of screws, second the most popular screw was technically up to speed, finally the concept of a standard screw. Sellers believed that this was a much broader issue than just the problem of too many types of screws. Sellers believed that there should be the concept of standards for certain types of parts with screws being the most obvious and important at the time. It is really important to understand that there were no standards prior to this time. It would be like

1

going into Home Depot or Lowes and the entire store would be filled with row after row of different types of proprietary screws.

Sellers came up with a standard screw proposal that he was going to present to others in manufacturing at a talk in Philadelphia. The name of talk Sellers gave on April 12, 1864, was called, "On a Uniform System of Screw Threads."[3] Sellers proposed that not only should there be standards, but there should be a standard screw, and it should be his screw. You can imagine the brains and courage it took in order to make this type of suggestion in 1864. It was truly a quantum leap in manufacturing. There were a number of problems that Sellers knew he had to address, so he proactively worked to mitigate these problems before making his proposal.

The most popular screw was the British Standard Whitworth (BSW), known as the Whitworth screw created by Joseph Whitworth in 1841.[4] Standardizing the screw was going to take a battle. The battle would not just focus on the detail of whether the Sellers screw was technically better than the Whitworth screw, but the larger question of why should standards even exist? Sellers was brilliant in that he went to the customers first to win their support for both the concept of a standard screw and why his screw was better.

The technical differences were important for manufacturers to understand. In the *Wired* article, Mr. Surowiecki points out, "These differences may sound minor, but in practical terms they were revolutionary. The 55-degree angle of Whitworth's screw was difficult to measure accurately without specially designed gauges. By contrast, Sellers' 60-degree thread—one angle of an equilateral triangle—could be measured with ease."

There was a meeting where Sellers shared his views on the importance of both a better screw design and the importance of having a standard screw. Sellers had done his homework and had already convinced four of the biggest machine shops to start using his screw at the time of his speech. This is how you address the chicken and egg problem regarding any new standard—follow the money and go to the end users. When the end users start demanding a standard and putting it in their requirements, vendors will have to adjust or die. The adoption of the Sellers screw occurred when a committee analyzed both screws and determined the Sellers screw was technically superior to the Whitworth screw.

The process of standardization is always a political struggle, with winners and losers. The primary winners will be those companies that understand it is co-opetition (competition and cooperation) that drives thriving markets. The primary losers will be those companies holding on to proprietary solutions at all costs. With a standard screw, you could now have standard tools, standard assembly lines, and the growth of mass production. I love the William Sellers story because it shows how a small standard can make such a huge and long lasting change. I believe MTConnect will end up in that same category of manufacturing significance.

When we first started seriously working on the MTConnect standard back in early 2007 at the University of California, Berkeley, the suggestion of co-opetition was first framed in the context of the Java Community Process (JCP). It is important to understand how manufacturing continues to evolve around co-opetition.

Co-opetition is the merging of two words: cooperation and competition. This is not new to manufacturing, but the full adoption of this concept is not always embraced in manufacturing. Too often I hear from a small subset of manufacturing equipment providers that they will support MTConnect when their customers demand it. While I certainly understand and appreciate that logic, I always ask them the following question: "If you posed the question to your

3

customer, would you rather have a proprietary way to get information from our machine tool or an open standard, which do you think they would select?" The response I always get back is, "Well of course they would want the open interface." I then reply, "So why don't you offer MTConnect then?"

The important points to remember are that while the idea of standards was very controversial, it proved to be brilliant because something as simple as a standard screw created many, many industries.

When individuals ask me, "What is so special about MTConnect if it is just an easy and open way to get information off of manufacturing equipment?" I explain how MTConnect provides a standard way for all manufacturing equipment to communicate and how standards can have a creative and amplifying effect for entire industries.

Over 18 percent of everything made in the world is made in the United States of America making America the global leader in manufacturing. Surprised? Probably not if you are someone who reads AMT's IMTS Insider or if you work in manufacturing. However, I would bet if you asked individuals, who are not in manufacturing, "Which country leads the world in manufacturing?" their answer would likely be China. As of 2010, China is second in global production, making 17.6 percent of the world's goods according to the National Association of Manufacturers (NAM). You might then enter into a long discussion about politics or the price of labor. I will not digress into that discussion here. Instead I would encourage everyone to listen to a short podcast by the National Public Radio (NPR) show on Planet Money called The Friday Podcast: Buttons and Other Connectors.[5]

The podcast drives home a very simple point that is sometimes forgotten in manufacturing—it is **not** lean manufacturing, it is **innovative** technology. Don't get me wrong, the principles of lean are important, but if you are not innovating, being lean is simply a race to the bottom. How much do you spend on research and development (R&D)? It always blows my mind when I hear someone in manufacturing say that there is not a lot to be gained by investing in R&D.

The NPR podcast compares and contrasts two companies. As NPR states on their Planet Money home page:

"Back in the day, the Buttonwood Corporation ran double shifts at its New York City factory, with 150 machines cranking out tens of thousands of buttons. These days, Chinese factories not only have cheaper labor, but also newer, fancier machines. Buttonwood—a family business, owned by two brothers—has just one employee left. They sell small orders of wood buttons, and take orders online at woodbuttons.com.

"The Zierick Manufacturing Corporation makes products that are all around us, but we never notice. Little pieces of metal that connect electronics components to control panels. This sounds like the kind of cheap, commodity item that would be made in a country with dramatically lower labor costs. But it isn't; Zierick's factory is in upstate New York. Zierick's trick is to keep coming up with new, patentable ideas to make connectors better and better. So if you want a really good, reliable connector, it's worth it to pay more and get one from them. The company's doing well. They have lots of employees, lots of customers. They just have to keep coming up with new ideas to stay ahead of everybody else."

The companies that are innovating and growing do not get the respect they deserve because most people believe American manufacturing is dead. In today's sound-bite news world this is not surprising. Tell your non-manufacturing friends who is winning and why in manufacturing. Finally, when you listen to this broadcast, you can see the difference between someone who is looking forward and innovating and someone who is looking at years gone by. As Scott McNealy, co-founder of Sun Microsystems would say, "Sometimes you are the windshield and sometimes you're the bug. Innovate and be the windshield. It is much better being the windshield than being the bug."

Brooks' Law

In all industries there are seminal books that are in the must-read category as someone is learning their trade. In manufacturing, one of these must-read books is *The Goal* by Eliyahu M. Goldratt and Jeff Cox. My favorite computer book dealing with the challenges of getting a product out the door is the Pulitzer Prize-winning book by Tracy Kidder called *The Soul of a New Machine.* In the computer industry there are numerous must-read books and certainly Frederick P. Brooks' *The Mythical Man-Month* written in 1975 and revised in 2012 is in that category. The lessons from Brooks' *The Mythical Man-Month* can also be applied to manufacturing. This is especially true as software becomes more important in manufacturing each and every day. "Brooks' Law," which is the focus of his book, is implicit in the other two books as well.

Here is the essence of Brooks' Law. When management makes the decision to throw more people at a software project that is running late, they do so under the firm belief that adding more people is the right and obvious decision to make at that point. The problem is that it is usually the wrong decision. Brooks' Law states, "adding manpower to a late software project makes it later."[6] At first glance, this may seem counter-intuitive. The reason Brooks' Law is usually right are multiple. I use the term "usually" here because there are exceptions to Brooks' Law. The reasons Brooks' Law usually holds up are when you bring new software developers onto a project there are a number of tasks that simply must be done. These include:

- Bringing new developers up-to-speed on the project. This typically involves current software developers and project leads investing time with these new developers.

- There might be training for the new developers because the software tools or practices the project is utilizing are different than what they have previously worked on. It is also can be a challenge integrating the new software developers into the existing communication framework.

- Dividing the work among the existing and new software developers is daunting, especially prioritizing the remaining work so the experienced developers are taking on the most difficult parts of the project.

- This partitioning of work can be extremely difficult if the initial architecture was not cleanly laid out separating interfaces from implementations.

What I mean by an "interface" is how one communicates with a piece of software. This is typically at a high level. For example, let's say I want to verify that when a prototype part is being created on a specific machine tool, it is being created by a category of machinists that represents the best in our company. I also want to make sure that these machinists are using a cutting tool that meets certain quality requirements my company has determined will be used for all prototype parts. What is the software interface I use to make this happen? In other words, how does a software application determine who is the best machinist and that we are using a specific cutting tool? Where does this information exist in digital format? Or, is this just in the shift manager's brain and not even written down anywhere? Side note—this is where an open and royalty-free protocol such as MTConnect provides simple interfaces to get information.

The "implementation" is the low-level set of specifics on what happens and how it happens.

Here's another way to think about the interface vs. implementation definitions in layman's terms. The interface for me to get the yard mowed on a Saturday is to yell at one of my three sons, "Get the yard mowed tonight, before it gets dark." If I do not hear anything from them in 14.896 femtoseconds, I then yell, "Are we clear?" If I hear a positive response, then I consider the task done. The implementation is my son going out to the shed, checking the gas in the John Deere tractor and the Honda push mower, then deciding whether he wants to mow the front or back yard first, and finally getting the yard mowed. I don't care how he mows the yard; just get the yard mowed before it gets dark. If time was tight, I could ask John to mow the back, Michael to mow the front, and have Tim trim. However, if I needed my half acre mowed in less than three minutes, the portioning and coordination to make this happen would be an interesting exercise. This portioning can be easy to do when it comes to a simple task such as mowing the yard when you can simply yell at one of your sons to get it done, but it is very hard for a software project that could require writing hundreds of thousands of lines or more of code.

Brooks also states in his book, "the man-month as a unit for measuring the size of a job is a dangerous and deceptive myth—it implies that men and months are interchangeable." It is well known that your gifted software developers can literally be 10x as productive as other software developers. This makes the dividing up of work even trickier.

A humorous statement that Brooks would make to drive home this point is, "the bearing of a child takes nine months, no matter how many women are assigned." This does drive home the point that some things just take time to make, and software is certainly in that category.

Have things changed since 1975 with software development? Absolutely. It used to be that everyone thought software should be developed like a boat going down a gentle waterfall. In other words, one went from planning to coding to component test to system test and finally to deployment in a nice logical fashion. Today all the realists know that software development needs to be agile, lean, have a clear portioning of tasks, and most importantly be interactive with the end customers. The type of computer languages have also changed a great deal enabling more portioning of tasks. When you think about the time frame of 1975 and computing, it is pretty remarkable to realize that even now Brooks' Law is still true many more times than it is false.

Missing Creativity in Our Schools and Manufacturing

Creative teachers in schools, creative instructors in business, or creative mentors in any walk of life can make all the difference in the world. We know this is true, yet we shackle our teachers in the classrooms and complain about how hard it is to find good people in business. I would argue it is not a lack of good teachers or a lack of smart workers—it is a lack of creative thinking by school administrators, teachers' union leaders, politicians, and business leaders that is the real problem.

The statistics are well known inside manufacturing when it comes to how difficult it is to find and keep good, qualified workers. President Obama has stated that there are over 600,000 well paying manufacturing jobs that are unfilled because of lack of qualified labor. I hear this all the time when I speak to leaders in manufacturing. The importance of having creative and well educated employees in manufacturing is growing each and every day. This is a huge problem in manufacturing, and it warrants discussion in a book on MTConnect and technology because what MTConnect enables is new and completely different ways to think about manufacturing. It's not just about education; it's about manufacturing creating an educational foundation with a petri-dish mindset. A petri-dish mindset means giving your employees the freedom to fail. Failure is good when it ignites creativity.

In the book *Imagine: How Creativity Works*, by Jonah Lehrer, he recites a survey of teachers who were asked about student creativity.[7] One hundred percent of the teachers stated they wanted creative students. When the same teachers were asked about traits that were important to them, a very high percent stated the exact opposite. These teachers said conforming and listening were the most important traits they wanted to see in their students. The teachers clearly did not want students speaking up and challenging them. I once worked at a company where a sales VP had physically removed the door from his office to prove he had an open-door policy. What was most ironic about this individual is that he had a reputation as the most closed-mind individual in the entire office. How often do we hear leaders state they are for education and creativity only to refute it with their actions? Is it being purposely disingenuous or is it ignorance?

When my youngest son Tim was in elementary school I asked him at the dinner table how the Standards of Learning (SOL) tests went that day for him. He responded, "My stomach hurt." My first reaction was to think that his teacher had said something to the class that put unnecessary pressure on the students and in particular Tim. When I asked him, "Why did your stomach hurt?" He told me something that exemplifies what is wrong with our education system. Tim said, "the principal said that kids do better on tests when they have breakfast, so we all had to eat breakfast—again." Tim went on to say, "I told them that I had already eaten a big breakfast, but my teacher said I had to eat again anyway so the principal would not get mad and that is why my stomach hurt."

The United States is ranked 27th in the world in mathematics and 22nd in science according to the 2009 Organization for Economic Co-operation and Development (OECD) Survey. Note that OECD does these surveys every three years and as of this writing, the 2012 surveys were not available. There are many reasons for United States' poor ranking. What is clearly not the problem is the amount of money spent per student. We spend twice as much as other countries. The problem is that we are not spending that money on getting the best teachers and teachers' unions are very reluctant to get rid of the bad teachers. Finland is ranked number one in both math and science. There is a very interesting article written by Stuart Conway for the *Smithsonian Magazine* in September 2011 titled, "Why Are Finland's Schools Successful?"[8] The first step was a conscious decision in 1963 to use education as the means to an economic recovery. "The second critical decision came in 1979," the article states, "when reformers required that every teacher earn a fifth-year master's degree in theory and practice at one of eight state universities—at state expense. From then on, teachers were effectively granted equal status with doctors and lawyers. Applicants began flooding teaching programs, not because the salaries were so high but because autonomy and respect made the job attractive." Think about that for a second—doctors, lawyers, and teachers were all on equal status. To even apply to be a teacher in Finland teachers must graduate in the top 10 percent of their class.

I was initially all for SOLs until my sister, who is a high school guidance counselor, as well as a licensed counselor and has a bachelor's, two master's, and a Ph.D. told me, "just watch what happens—teachers will teach to the test." I was 100 percent wrong on SOLs, and my sister was 100 percent right. Teachers teach to the test, and creativity be damned. In the same *Smithsonian Magazine* article, there is a great section on the fallacy of standardized tests. "Finnish educators have a hard time understanding the United States' fascination with standardized tests. 'Americans like all these bars and graphs and colored charts,' Louhivuori teased, as he rummaged through his closet looking for past years' results. 'Looks like we did better than average two years ago,' he said after he found the reports. 'It's nonsense. We know much more about the children than these tests can tell us.'"

Heaven Is A Playground is the name of my favorite sports book by the famous author Rick Telander. This is a fantastic and award-winning book about Telander spending the summer in Brooklyn coaching a youth summer basketball team. The title of the book comes from a quote by author G.K. Chesterton, "The true object of all human life is play. Earth is a task garden; heaven is a playground."[9] The problem for the United States is that we have turned schools into task gardens and teachers into robots. As parents and professionals we know this is not a hard problem to solve. Hire the best and get out of their way. It is the same in any industry. When I hear a teachers' union leader state, "it is very hard to rate which teachers are the best," I have to say that is complete and utter nonsense. I think about when my wife and I were walking one of our three sons to the bus stop on their first day of school. A parent with an older child would ask, "Who does your son have this year as a teacher?" When we replied you could instantly tell whether or not your child got the best teacher. With a cross section of parents you could find out which are the great teachers and which ones are not. Students obviously know as well. I have the utmost respect for teachers and guidance counselors, but just not politicians and teachers union leaders who spend more time arguing than getting to work and making improvements.

In the Lehrer's *Imagine* book he talks about how Google borrowed the idea from 3M to allow employees to spend 15 percent of their time per week to work on their own projects of their own choosing. These were not projects that were unrelated to their jobs, but projects that the employees felt might have a substantial payoff in the future. In other words, there was some risk to these projects not having an immediate return on investment (ROI), but the risk allowed them to create and the payoff could be huge for the company and the employee. Some companies refer to this type of work as personal R&D. How many manufacturers are doing that? How many school systems? Right now some of you are likely thinking, "Well, that would be crazy to do for manufacturing!" Why would that be crazy? If you want an individual to be creative, then that person must have the time, freedom, and authority to try something completely new. This comes from the culture of the company. You can walk in a plant or shop and know within 10 minutes of talking to management what type of environment exists. Treat your employees like machines and they will act like machines.

President Obama mentioned manufacturing eight times in his State of the Union message in 2013. That is seven more times than President Bush did for all eight of his state of the union messages, but what has really changed? We keep hearing about the problem, but what are the creative educational solutions? I hear the same old solutions being brought out again and again with different results being hoped for. That is the definition of insanity. No disrespect to my generation, the 50+ year olds, but we are the wrong ones to be solving the problem of creative manufacturing education. I go to these manufacturing conferences and I can count the number of young people on one hand. True, I am old, so theoretically everyone is young compared to me, but I am talking about folks in their 20s. I would love to see a manufacturing conference where every person over 50 had to also bring two 20-somethings in manufacturing to the conference. There would be a session with young manufacturing folks on stage with a round table on creative education. It's worth a try in my humble opinion. There are some young folks, like Joel Neidig of Indiana Technology and Manufacturing Companies (ITAMCO), who are doing amazing things in manufacturing. ITAMCO is also working with a local high school to help students understand and appreciate manufacturing. There are a number of examples of both manufacturers and manufacturing equipment providers working with their local school systems. You can go get your free MTConnect app today for Apple or Android thanks to Joel. I wish we could clone Joel!

Everyone agrees that Steve Jobs was a genius at creativity, but few know what he did to create a creative environment. At Pixar he looked at creativity in the same way Darwin looked at evolution. You need the right environment and the right mix for new life to be created. Jobs changed the environment at Pixar, and here is how Jonah Lehrer tells it in his book *Imagine*. "The Pixar studios were largely designed by Steve Jobs. People at Pixar will often refer to the building as 'Steve's Movie.' And the original plan for the Pixar Studios called for three separate buildings. One building for the animators, one building for the computer scientists, one building for everyone else, the writers, directors, editors, and so on. Jobs took one look at this and said that's a terrible idea. He then insisted everyone be in the exact same space, because he realized the success of Pixar would depend on these cultures learning how to collaborate; getting the engineers and the computer scientists and the animators to work together, to learn from each other, to share knowledge."

The next time you are evaluating or creating an education program or determining how to best have a creative environment for your employees think about education in Finland and also ask yourself, "What would 3M, Google, or Steve Jobs do?"

Manufacturing's 3Ds

A statement made by John Engler, the president and CEO of the National Association of Manufacturers (NAM), keeps echoing in my mind. Mr. Engler spoke at the Emerging Technology Center (ETC) at International Manufacturing Technology Show (IMTS) 2010. Mr. Engler stated, "too often, people think of manufacturing as 3D [*as he looked back on the*

3D ETC Theater]—dark, dreary, and depressing. How many of you recommended that your children go into manufacturing?" I think a lot about what Mr. Engler said that morning. Mr. Engler then went on to discuss the exciting and cool aspects of manufacturing. He emphasized that the problem is the classic theory that "perception is reality." I could not agree more. I hear industry leaders in manufacturing bemoan the fact that there are very few young people who are entering manufacturing—even in today's economy. The question then becomes three-fold: 1) Can the 3D perception of manufacturing change? 2) What is really needed to drive the change? 3) What specifically needs to happen for young people to think manufacturing is an industry that is exciting, cool, pays well, and has a very bright future? Not easy questions to be sure.

I predict that we will see a transition from Mr. Engler's 3D to a new 3D in manufacturing. What is the new 3D? Dynamic, Digital, and Disruptive. If you think that I am just coming up with marketing mumbo-jumbo, please keep reading. Let me be clear, it won't be marketing that will drive this change. It won't be President Obama visiting a manufacturing plant. Although I am glad that the president is doing more for manufacturing than any president that I can remember. Let's face it, if the United States had let the auto industry die out, it would have been a disaster for our country and in particular manufac-turing. A point the president also understands is the importance of the entire manufacturing process, from design to distribution, and the slippery slope that occurs when manufacturing leaves a country—so many other aspects of manufacturing eventually follow. The president's emphasis on the entire art-to-part value chain seems to be a channeling of Doug Woods, current Association for Manufacturing Technology (AMT) president, and AMT's Manufacturing Mandate. Driving down the price of additive technology, in the exact same fashion as the advent of the PC, will be the key. Let's take a look back to see the similarities to the PC industry.

I first started working in the computer industry in 1978. In the 1970s and early 1980s it was fascinating to witness the entire PC revolution unfold from the introduction of the MITS Altair 8800 in 1975, Heathkit, Radio Shack's TRS-80, Apple-1, Commodore PET, the Atari, and of course the establishment of the personal computer with the IBM PC on August 12, 1981. It is important to remember who had access to computers prior to the introduction of these small, reasonably priced computers. Unless you or someone you knew was in the computer industry or you were attending college or university and majoring in Data Processing (that is what it was called before Computer Science), you had zero chance to ever getting your hands on a computer. The introduction of the low-cost computing for the masses was the foundation for the greatest generation of intellectual property and wealth this planet has ever seen. In Malcolm Gladwell's best-selling book, *Outliers: The Story of Success*, Gladwell states, "researchers have settled on what they believe is the magic number for true expertise: ten thousand hours."[10] Gladwell brings up example after example of young people who had the gift of access to technology and the passion to use it as those who ended up being the leaders of the computer revolution. Being smart was not the sole requirement, but instead it was those with easy access to technology, the passion to learn and experiment, as well as just plain hard work that was the difference in those that changed the world. It took 10,000 hours before those individuals were true experts.

I believe there is a better-than-even chance we will witness history repeat itself, to a lesser degree, with manufacturing for the masses. Let's think about the similarities. Five years ago, did the average person have the ability to actually manufacture something today? Not unless they were either in manufacturing or knew someone who was, they certainly did not. Yes, some schools provided basic machine tools, but it was not like those were easy to access for the masses. All that is changing with 3D printers.

Without question, the most exciting part of IMTS 2010 was the Emerging Technology Center (ETC). It was additive technology and the micro/nano technology that had everyone shaking their heads in amazement. The key will be additive technology and specifically 3D printers. The price of additive technology continues to drop. A great example of the start of this revolution is Maker Faire. Maker Faire is put on by *MAKE Magazine*. As Wikipedia states, "*Make* (or *MAKE*) is an American quarterly magazine focuses on do it yourself (DIY) and/or DIWO (Do It With Others) projects involving computers, electronics, robotics, metalworking, woodworking, and other disciplines. The magazine is marketed to people who enjoy 'making' things and features complex projects which can often be completed with cheap materials, including household items."[11] Another site to check out is www.thingiverse.com. It has a number of inexpensive additive technology devices and some interesting projects. Today, the state of this technology is in the equivalent to what was going on in the PC industry back in the mid-1970s. These technologies are viewed as cool stuff for the geeks who like to make DIY or DIWO.

There are a five pieces of the puzzle that are needed for this "manufacturing anywhere" revolution to occur. Four of these are already happening to various degrees.

1. **Free or inexpensive CAD/CAM software.** We are already there.

2. **Low-cost 3D printers.** This is the key piece that is starting to happen today to various degrees.

3. **Service bureaus.** The ability to easily send the CAD files to a local 3D printing service bureau that can make the part on a full production 3D printer. This is already

happening at 3D printing firms like Proto Cafe in Redwood City, California.

4. **Large additive technology companies and machine tool companies** that realize it is worth priming this pump because it serves their strategic interests.

5. **Everything connected on the net.** With MTConnect we are quickly adding manufacturing equipment to the enterprise. The machine tool is the network.

A great example of why this is important at the professional level is in Greenville, South Carolina, with a company called ADEX Machining Technologies. What is extremely impressive about ADEX is the new position they created. Traditionally, you have CNC programmers and machinists, which are separate positions. ADEX has created a hybrid role where employees must be accomplished CNC programmers *and* skilled machinists. ADEX employees have made it very clear that, by wearing both hats, it gives them the satisfaction of both designing parts and then actually creating the part. ADEX has a tremendous challenge in finding employees who can meet this new hybrid role.

Looking back at the PC revolution, we know the first phase was the ability to provide cheap computing to the masses and the second phase was when these low-cost systems were all networked. The PC revolution was dynamic, digital, and it was very disruptive to the status quo. The entrepreneurs who developed software on PCs and then eventually started their own companies sparked a revolution. Who will be the Bill Gates, the Steve Jobs, and the Scott McNealy (co-founder of Sun Microsystems) of manufacturing? I will bet that it will be those young people with access to technology, the passion to learn and experiment, as well as those who are just plain hard workers who will end up changing the world of manufacturing from old 3D to new 3D—dynamic, digital, and disruptive. I can't wait.

Chapter 2: Infusing Sun's DNA into Manufacturing

Not All the Smart People Work for You

I first heard Bill Joy, co-founder of Sun Microsystems, utter the sentence, "because not all the smart people work for you" back in the mid-1990s. He was asked why Sun was open-sourcing a particular software program. "Why would Sun work so hard to create a new piece of software and then make the source code available to anyone who wanted it?" That was the question being asked by the new Sun manager at a meeting. It seemed completely counter-intuitive to this new Sun employee. Why spend millions of dollars developing a piece of software to then give away the original source code? The manager was essentially questioning Sun's software business strategy. Bill was not being flip in his answer, but his short and concise answer could have easily been misinterpreted as being arrogant if you did not understand Sun's business strategy. Sun was not interested in short-term dollars, but instead interested in building a software platform that others would use as a foundation to build their products.

What exactly did Bill mean by the sentence "because not all the smart people work for you"? By opening up the software, other smart people at other companies can work with it and make it even more valuable. There are countless examples of this type of collaboration in the computer industry. From a business standpoint, it has to do with your primary objective and where you want to make your money. This also has a counter-intuitive premise that many in manufacturing find impossible to embrace. The premise is that by working with your competitors it can make your own company stronger.

Let's be clear, I am talking about collaborating on an open standard or platform. I am not talking about collusion, but

19

working together to define a standard interface and then compete for the implementation. MTConnect is a great example of collaboration. The MTConnect Institute set up its Working Groups in a similar fashion that Sun set up the Java Community Process (JCP) with the Java Specification Request (JSR) process. The basic idea is that you bring in industry experts to work together on an industry specification where all the involved companies have both business and technical interests. These companies cooperate to create a standard and then compete on the best implementation. The driving reason for doing this is that the old adage, "the great thing about standards is that there are so many of them," stifles innovation.

Collaboration does not mean that a company should not exercise common sense when sending individuals to these industry standard meetings. My father-in-law was general counsel for the Electronics Industry Association (EIA) and told me a few stories of members sending engineers to meetings where everyone else sent a lawyer. His analogy was that it was like bringing a knife to a gunfight—never a good idea. Usually, these industry meetings are the technical and business experts who are working together. It is also industry standard that there are legal agreements regarding intellectual property to protect both the standard and the individual companies.

Manufacturing in general is slow to adopt this "not all the smart people work for you" collaboration mentality because it is not how their dad or their grandfather did it. The logic is, "my grandfather drove a Cadillac, my dad drove a Cadillac, and I am driving a Cadillac, so why should I change?" While it is hard to argue with decades of success, one also needs to remember Darwin's advice, "In the struggle for survival, the fittest win out at the expense of their rivals because they succeed in adapting themselves best to their environment."[12] I would suggest that manufacturing is changing to be less proprietary, to be less closed, and to have a less "go at it alone" type of mentality. Manufacturing will model the computer industry where open wins and proprietary loses.

Today there are great examples of companies that embrace open collaboration and open thinking. It is certainly not a coincidence that companies that have great thought leaders on the business and technical sides of the house and have embraced MTConnect are doing very well. These industry leaders embraced MTConnect because they knew that MTConnect had a real chance to change manufacturing in tremendous ways, and most importantly, it was the open and correct choice for their respective businesses. These companies have been absolutely proven correct. Today, if you go to a machine tool company or a manufacturing equipment provider that understands what it means to be open they will make it easy for end users to find support for MTConnect and the steps needed to MTConnect-enable their legacy and current products. These companies are viewed as open and trusted advisors in manufacturing and they are taking away business from the closed and proprietary machine tool companies.

There are well over 100 companies that are either MTConnect Technical Advisory Group Members or MTConnect implementers and are active with MTConnect. In manufacturing, if you are not a member of MTConnect and actively supporting the standard, then you are viewed as being closed and proprietary. Being closed and proprietary in manufacturing is affecting sales now and the importance of being open will simply increase in the future as more and more companies embrace MTConnect. When I talk to some of the machine tool companies or control companies that have not yet embraced MTConnect, a standard response is typically, "well, we will get on MTConnect when everyone else has" or "not all of our customers are demanding MTConnect yet." Obviously, with that type thinking these companies will be late to the MTConnect open revolution and will pay a price in the marketplace. The problem for many of them is that it will be too little and too late. The companies that embraced MTConnect and open systems early will clean their closed and proprietary clocks in the marketplace.

If we look at the manufacturing companies that are embracing open thinking and open collaboration, these companies report secondary benefits in morale as their employees typically tell their management that they have much higher job satisfaction. You don't have to be an HR expert to appreciate the fact that employees who have an opportunity to work on something that is bigger than their day-to-day work is a plus. I know this is true because I experienced this myself and know many individuals who have stayed with a company because they were allowed and encouraged to do this type of industry collaboration work. This can provide your more senior employees interesting career growth opportunities.

The next time you are considering how to attack a problem or whether or not your company should participate in an industry standard such as MTConnect, think back to Bill Joy's advice and remember, "not all the smart people work for you." You might be pleasantly surprised with the results.

The Culture of "Open Systems for Open Minds™"

That phrase was my all-time favorite slogan at Sun Microsystems. It might seem obvious that everyone should want an open system, but as it turns out, this does not always prove to be true. An open system is open or closed depending on the industry, the time period, the context, as well as the organization supporting the system.

In the computer industry, open or closed is better defined than manufacturing. What I mean by this is that if you ask someone in the computer industry the question, "What does it mean to be an open system?" The answers you will receive will likely be along the lines of, "an open computer system is one that has an operating system with its source code out in the open and public, uses the most popular and open programming languages, uses standard interfaces that are open and royalty-free, and this makes it portable between architectures." If you were speaking to someone who has been in the computer industry a long time, the answer would be very short and simple such as, "a Unix or Linux box."

What about the time period? If we were to go back to the 1960s and early 1970s, open computing would not have been a common term. Terms such as IBM plug-compatible would have been the definition of open. Plug-compatible meant that you could take a board from an older mainframe and use it in the backplane of a new computer of that same vendor. In 1981 IBM announced the IBM PC and created, some would argue by mistake, an open hardware platform where the terms IBM PC-compatible and PC-compatible meant it could run the same OS and software as the IBM PC, but typically would be a less expensive system. The IBM PC was viewed as an open system in the 1980s with Microsoft's DOS. In the 1980s, Sun Microsystems redefined open systems with the introduction of the SPARC platform where other companies could not only make systems that could use the SPARC processors, but companies could manufacture their own SPARC processors. In the 1990s the Linux operating system redefined the word open and that definition still stands today. Linux is a completely open operating system that was created by Linus Torvalds and released to the world on October 5, 1991, in open source form while Linus was a student at the University of Helsinki. Linux is the most popular open operating system on planet earth today. It literally runs on every type of computer that most people could name and many types of devices on which you did not even realize there was an operating system. Linux won because it was open and free.

How about context? This gives meaning to both the industry and the time period discussions. For example, is Apple an open system? Is Microsoft an open system? Is Oracle an open system? How about Google? How about iOS versus Android? It could be argued that Microsoft is more open than Apple in 2013. Microsoft provides developers with much more information and tools than Apple does. A better example is from an operating system standpoint. Where can I buy an Apple clone? The answer to that is "nowhere." How about an IBM-PC clone? "Anywhere" is the correct answer. Apple's Mac OS X is based on Unix, but no one considers Mac OS X an open operating system such as Linux in 2013. Oracle has both open systems, they own MySQL and Java, and they also own closed systems. Oracle believes this is best for their business and it is hard to argue with Oracle's tremendous success. Oracle might argue that they are an open company because they publish their interfaces, so they are an open platform. Open means many things to many people. An open interface simply means that I tell you how to "talk" to my software or how to access my data. For example, if you want to write your own software to talk to an Oracle database, the instructions on how a software developer would do that would be made available. Being available does not mean free because there could be a fee for this privilege. Many think of Google as being the anti-Microsoft and being open, but are they really? It depends. Are we talking about source code or data? The point here is that MTConnect is open, royalty-free, and open source. This was done by design and it is a key reason it has been so successful.

We discussed open systems in the context of the software or the instructions that cause a computer to act. Now, let's talk about open access to data. Is Facebook open? Not from a data standpoint, and it should not be open. That model works for them because they have a closed-garden approach that makes sense. How about Twitter? I can search Twitter at http://twitter.com/search. Does access to data make it open or closed? As you can see, context changes everything.

The other aspect of context is the organization behind the system. The Association for Manufacturing Technology (AMT) has been the key driving and supporting force behind MTConnect from the very beginning. Specifically, Paul Warndorf, vice president of manufacturing technology at AMT, has been the key person driving MTConnect. Don't get me wrong, lots of folks, yours truly included, have helped out a great deal, but you must have a singular driving force controlling the money and the vision. AMT has invested literally a seven-figure amount in MTConnect, not because of any hidden revenue stream for AMT, but rather because it was the right thing for their members and, more importantly, it was the right thing for manufacturing. Sun Microsystems had Scott McNealy as the guiding visionary for doing things the right way at Sun. It was impossible to overstate the importance of Scott to Sun Microsystems. MTConnect has Paul Warndorf. When companies and individuals look at a given technology, the organization and the individuals in that organization play a large role in the determination of the overall motive behind a given system. While motivation can sometimes be difficult to ascertain, when it is a 501(c)(6) non-profit, as both AMT and the MTConnect Institute are, the questions become less probing on real intentions. This does not mean that we do not receive probing questions at the MTConnect Institute, but they are usually more quickly accepted when the person realizes we are not for profit.

Manufacturing is moving to open systems with MTConnect, but there is still an ocean of different definitions of what an open system really is in the world of manufacturing. For example, when I was at the International Manufacturing Technology Show (IMTS) 2012, I asked exactly that question—"What is an open system in the world of manufacturing?"—of those who came to the Emerging Technology Center (ETC) and the exhibitors I visited while I walked the show floor. The answers I received were quite interesting. In the software area, if I was talking to a vendor who was a member of the MTConnect Institute, the answers were more in-line with what you would expect in the computer industry. However, if I spoke to someone who was not a member of the MTConnect Institute, the answers gave me flashbacks to the 1970s. This is not meant to be a derogatory statement, just a reflection of the importance industry, context, and time period for manufacturing. A common example of the answers I received is "the ability to pay for the manual, license, and software development kit in order to access the proprietary Application Programming Interfaces (APIs)." APIs are the defined methods or procedures that a software company will list as the mechanism to either use their software or access their data. An example might be the need for a random number for a game that is being written for a smartphone. Instead of the software developer writing a random number generator, the software company might have a random generator method that would simply be called or used. This saves software developers time so they do not have to reinvent the wheel. The less code they have to write, the more productive they are and the less chance to introduce bugs. Another example of an API would be the instructions on how to access data from a database. There is no one in the computer industry that would define an open system as simply making the APIs available in the year 2013.

This is not to say that a closed model might not be what is best for a given company. Look at Apple. For anyone who owns Apple stock, they are very pleased to have stock in a closed system. This is true if they did not purchase Apple when it was at over $700 a share. I own lots of Apple products. I am writing this on a MacBook Pro with an iPhone 5 in my pocket right now with a Mac mini in my home office. I have purchased three iPads for family members, and I have lost track of the number of iPhones and iPods I have purchased over the years. But, that is not the point of the more interesting question which is: "Will iPhone still be the phone to have in five years or will Android be the absolute hands-down dominant platform?" It has been stated that Android out-ships iPhone by almost four to one today, so what will it be in five years? Who knows, but the key point is that Android is based on an open platform and Apple is not. Go try to create an iPhone clone and let me know how that works for you. Customers like open systems because it gives them choice. But, why do some companies like Apple do so well? They innovate, and their systems just work, as one would expect. Apple will need to out-innovate and out-integrate the entire Android cast of players. That is easy to say, but very hard to do.

What does the future for manufacturing hold in terms of open systems? There have been other attempts at open systems in manufacturing besides MTConnect that had very limited results. Those efforts might have been affected by limited resources and limited vision. I do believe we will continue to see manufacturing embrace open systems. Not because of any altruistic reason, but because it makes good economic sense. The challenge with entirely closed systems is that you must place all the bets correctly. If you do, then you can win big. If you miss any of those bets, changing platforms might be your death knell. Open systems are on a continuum and the industry, the time period, the context, as well as the organization supporting the system all matter when coming to the conclusion of whether the system is truly open, partially open, basically closed, or completely proprietary.

Hang on folks, because the next five years in manufacturing will be quite interesting. I am going to borrow one of Sun Microsystem's best slogans and state, "Open Manufacturing for Open Minds." Sounds like something I need to put on a t-shirt.

The Network Is the Computer™

The phrase, "The Network Is the Computer," was Sun Microsystems' company tag line. Today, that phrase is obvious to anyone who has ever sat in front of a web browser; however, in 1984 that was the most prophetic statement anyone could have made to predict the future of computing. I worked at Sun from early 1987 through 2010 and this slogan proved to be the blueprint not only for Sun's vision of computing, but the vision of computing for companies around the globe. It is important to understand how and why this slogan came to be a landmark for an entire industry.

The history of this phrase goes back to a 1984 train ride in China with John Gage—Sun employee #21, creator of the JavaOne conference and NetDay (which provided Internet access and technology to hundreds of thousands of public school classrooms), and chief researcher and director of the Science Office—and Bill Joy, Sun co-founder and chief scientist, also called the "Edison of the Internet" by *Fortune Magazine*. How do I know this? I was fortunate enough to have a number of dinners with John and Bill. I remember asking Bill at a sushi restaurant in Aspen, Colorado, how the phrase came about. Bill told the story that he and John were traveling on the train in China and they were going through John's slides. John made the observation that importance of the network was growing at an exponential rate, and he wanted to reflect that in the title of his upcoming talk. Initially, John said, "the network is the disk drive," to which Bill, replied that the phrase did not capture his talk. John then came up with, "the network is the computer," and that was used for the talk and became Sun's famous tag line.

A few years later I was having dinner with John and a chief technology officer from a local company in Washington, DC, when I decided to ask John about the history of Sun's tag line. John repeated what Bill said almost word for word.

It is very important to put that time period in perspective for those who were not in the industry back then. In 1984 computer networking was just starting to take shape with various non-compatible networks that completely lacked the characteristics that we take for granted today. In the 1980s and the early 1990s there were different topologies from ring, star, bus, and net to the plethora of networks and protocols from AppleTalk, Banyan VINES, FDDI, SMB, MS-NET, Ethernet, Token Ring, DECnet, SNA, ARCnet, 802.3, SDLC, XNS, X.25, TCP/IP, ISDN, and ATM to name just a few. Networking computers together was complicated and expensive. A popular network was called SneakerNet. For those of you not old enough, SneakerNet was when you grabbed a floppy, wrote the file(s) needed to be transferred on it, and then carried it (SneakerNet) to the person's PC that needed the file. The role of network engineer came out of this time period. There was no plug-n-play as we have today. There was no cloud computing. There were no smartphones. There were no iPads or tablets. AOL was considered a powerhouse in the early 1990s because they had literally banks of modems that you would dial into and hear the high-pitch hand shake between your computer's modem and AOL's on the other end. For John Gage to have made that incredible, insightful comment in 1984 is absolutely amazing.

Digital Equipment Corporation (DEC) came out with a t-shirt that said, "The Network Is the Network, The Computer Is the Computer, Sorry for Any Confusion." At Sun, we got a kick out of that t-shirt, but DEC really did miss the point.

Today, the phrase is ingrained in everything that we do online. When you use an app on your iPhone or Android, do you know all of the software that runs? Do you even care where the data is stored? Not unless you are a geek you don't. You simply want access to your data in a fast and reliable fashion.

On January 10, 2006, I happened to be out at Sun's Headquarters in Menlo Park, California, when I heard about the Sun Founders' Panel to be held the following evening at The Computer History Museum. Like any long-time Sun employee or geek in general, I wanted to be there live and was able to go. It was a fantastic night that was hosted by John Gage with all four of Sun's founders there—Andy Bechtolsheim, Vinod Khosla, Scott McNealy, and Bill Joy. I learned about Vaughn Pratt, professor emeritus at Stanford who directed the SUN workstation project at Stanford from 1980 to 1982 out of which Sun Microsystems' first workstations were based.

 Vaughn even designed the famous ambigram Sun logo, which features four interleaved copies of the word "sun."

At the end of the evening, there was time for questions and answers. I thought this was a great time to permanently capture the story of "The Network Is the Computer." I went to the microphone and asked Bill and John to retell the story, which they did.

As you can probably tell by now, I am a bit of history buff when it comes to the computer industry. I believe how we got to a given point matters. I also believe that the computer industry is one of the best examples of where a rising tide really does lift all ships. When John made his famous statement it was not just a title for his talk in China, nor was simply the future tag line of Sun Microsystems, but it was really a call to action for an entire industry. By laying out the destination, John inspired thousands of engineers from around the globe to help build that vision.

In 2006, I was giving a keynote at AMT's annual meeting in Lake Las Vegas, Nevada. This was the first of two keynotes that sparked the creation of MTConnect. Dr. David Patterson of University of California, Berkeley, gave the second keynote laying out MTConnect. In my presentation I borrowed Sun's slogan and modified it to make a point regarding the future of manufacturing. My slide title was, "The Network Is the Machine Tool." I strongly believed that then, and time has only reinforced my belief.

Chapter 3: A Manufacturing Revolution

Three Days at IMTS

As president and chairman of the board for the MTConnect Institute, I get asked all the time: "How did MTConnect come about?" It is a story that I love telling, and it clearly demonstrates why the Association for Manufacturing Technology (AMT) is such an exceptional association.

Let me provide a little history to give this story some context. I first worked with AMT when my next-door neighbor, Peter Eelman, vice president of exhibitions and the person who runs the International Manufacturing Trade Show (IMTS), asked me if I could give a keynote on the Internet in 2000. AMT had lost a keynote speaker and their conference was just three weeks away. Peter is a great guy, fantastic neighbor, a real manufacturing industry icon, and a true friend, so of course I would move my schedule to help him and AMT out. Plus, it did not hurt that it was in Puerto Rico and they paid for my wife Julie to attend as well. My talk went well and it was at this Annual Meeting in 2000 that I first met all the great folks at AMT.

In March 2006, AMT asked me to come up with a speaker from Sun Microsystems who was specifically in Sun's manufacturing organization to speak at AMT's Annual Meeting in Lake Las Vegas. I went through three such speakers over a six-month period as each one either left Sun on their own or had their position eliminated. After the third speaker left the company, I was out of manufacturing candidates. I felt embarrassed for both Sun and myself that I let AMT down. When I apologized to John Byrd, AMT's president at that time, for not being able to deliver a Sun speaker, John suggested that I do the keynote. I was more than happy to do this, but I wanted to invest the time to do a great job for AMT. John came up with a great suggestion: I could spend three days at IMTS 2006 with AMT's chief technology officer and vice president of technology, Paul Warndorf, in preparation for the keynote. It was a brilliant idea, and I jumped at it. John and Paul are both great guys and true thought leaders in manufacturing. Paul has forgotten more about manufacturing than I will ever know in my entire life. Paul took me around to countless exhibitors to learn about the different technologies and ask questions about them. With decades of computer systems experience under my belt and a limitless resource of manufacturing knowledge by my side, I was able to examine the manufacturing industry in a new way.

As the old Chinese proverb says, "If you want to know what water is, don't ask the fish." While the pace of networked technologies has only accelerated outside of the manufacturing pond, within the manufacturing industry I saw a great need for technological advancement.

After we finished the two days, I met with John and Paul and made two specific observations and two suggestions.

My observations:

1. Manufacturing does not have a manufacturing problem. Manufacturing has a computer science problem. The manufacturing industry was like the computer industry back in the mid-1980s. There were too many network protocols, and the fight was to own the winning protocol. Back then it was very expensive and you had to place a bet on which network protocol was going to win. It could easily be an additional $700 to enable your PC to be networked in the enterprise. Eventually, a standard communicator was selected when Transmission Control Protocol/Internet Protocol (TCP/IP) Ethernet won the network battle. When this happened the number of computers networked grew by

multitudes, as did the software that would take advantage of the ubiquitous networking. It was the classic story of a rising tide lifting all ships.

2. Until you have an open and royalty-free way for these machine tools to speak to the rest of the world, the knowledge needed to ensure innovation, quality, and growth will continue to be elusive; and manufacturing will just continue to struggle. The technologies are already out there today with XML, http, and TCP/IP. There is no need to reinvent the wheel. A usable solution could be built on the *de facto* Internet platform that already exists. Additionally, it would be important to avoid charging for the protocol and for each deployment, as this approach would hamper overall industry improvement that could be gained through open collaboration.

My suggestions:

1. You need an economic wakeup call on why it is important to have an open and royalty-free way for these machine tools to speak to the rest of the world.

2. You need someone who has led a revolution or two, since this is what we are really talking about.

They asked me whom I suggested. I said the only person I would recommend would be Dr. David Patterson of the University of California, Berkeley (UCB). Dave Patterson is a computer pioneer and a true legend in the computer industry. Dave is one of the most recognizable names in computer science. I knew Dave because he was the advisor at UCB to Bill Joy. If you recall, Bill was a co-founder at Sun and has been called "the Edison of the Internet" by *Fortune Magazine*. Bill is a legendary programmer and system visionary. I also knew Dave from working with him when I was chairman of a futures conference Sun Microsystems held in 2000 that was called SE

Symposium 2000 with the marketing phrase, "Catching Waves in the New Millennium." As chair of the futures track, I basically had unlimited funds to get whatever speakers I wanted. The reason I say basically unlimited is because in 2000 Sun Microsystems was riding the dotcom bubble, and we were flush with cash and sales. That would not last however. That is a different story to tell. I came up with a list of individuals in the computer industry I had always wanted to meet. Dave Patterson was on the top of that list.

John Byrd asked if I would reach out to Dave Patterson. Luckily, Dave agreed to work on the project provided I come out and brief him and that we work together on both presentations. I was thrilled to work with someone of Dave Patterson's stature. It was like being a high school basketball player and having Michael Jordan say he wants to work closely with you.

On October 14, 2006, my parents asked me to go to the U.S. Air Force Memorial Dedication Ceremony with them. My father was in the Air Force for almost 30 years.

Figure 2. *The author at the U.S. Air Force Memorial Dedication Ceremony on October 14, 2006.*

As we were waiting for the VIPs to get there to speak, I walked up to the folks standing around the F-35 and asked the question of the F-35 Team: "What was the biggest challenge you had in the design of the Joint Strike Fighter?"

Their answer: "Everything was designed on the computer and the biggest challenge we had was interoperability of data. We were forced to use the same type of PC, the same OS, the same application, because we could not depend on the ability to reliably exchange data if we did not. This added time and complexity to the overall process."

The importance of a common data format cannot be understated in manufacturing. The National Institute of Standards and Technology (NIST) has stated that data compatibility costs manufacturing billions of dollars per year.

Dave Patterson and I worked very hard together to create two hour-long keynote speeches. Dave joked that if he knew how much time he was going to put into it, he might not have said yes to me. But our presentations were a huge success. Rick Kline, Sr., of Gardner Communications came up to us afterwards and said that our presentations were two of the best that he had ever seen in manufacturing. It was great to see that we'd had such a positive impact.

In Figure 3, you can see my picture on the left and Dr. David Patterson of UCB on the right as we appeared in AMT's 2006 Annual Meeting literature. The theme of the meeting was "Manufacturing in the Internet Age."

Figure 3. *Dave Edstrom (top left), Dave Patterson (top right), and a poster from AMT's 2006 Annual Meeting.*

Dr. Patterson's talk was titled: "Creating a Thriving American Manufacturing Base in 21st Century America," and my talk was titled, "How the Internet's Participation Age Will Drive Dramatic Changes in the Machine Tool Industry."

Doug Woods was AMT's chairman of the board at the time, leading AMT along with then-president John Byrd. John and Doug are both thought-leaders for all of manufacturing, and their support of MTConnect at the very beginning was absolutely critical. John and Doug suggested that AMT seriously consider our proposal for a common way for machine tools to speak using proven Internet protocols. I told my wife that night that I felt great about what Dave Patterson and I had accomplished, but I was not convinced a manufacturing association had the courage to execute this plan to revolutionize manufacturing. It requires a great deal of passion, expertise, money, and courage to stick with creating and driving a standard in such a proprietary industry. The effort needed to truly create and sustain a revolution such as MTConnect is unbelievable. You need an organization like AMT to continue to support it. Many other similar efforts in manufacturing and the computer industry that have stalled and died, because organizations behind them totally underestimated the effort and time needed.

John Byrd, Doug Woods, and Paul Warndorf proved me wrong in terms of AMT's courage and leadership. In November, just one month after the 2006 AMT Annual Meeting, a small group of us went to meet with Dave Patterson at UCB. Dave brought in Dr. Armando Fox, from the Computer Science Department, to help lead this effort. Paul brought in Dr. Dave Dornfeld of UCB's Mechanical Engineering Department to join the MTConnect team. Armando later brought in Will Sobel, who was an assistant professor at UCB.

It was Will that did the real heavy lifting with MTConnect. It was Will who put countless hours into leading the efforts to create the actual spec and writing the adapters, agents, demos, and so many things for MTConnect. Will continues to do a lot of the heavy lifting today, but his time is also spent running his new company, System Insights. Will Sobel is the chief architect of MTConnect and there are not enough words in this book that could describe his incredible contributions. MTConnect would have never happened without his expertise, passion, and guidance. Paul Warndorf has been MTConnect's shepherd, conductor, and guiding light. Paul has been there from day one. Paul has the decades of contacts in manufacturing and in government that have made the adoption of MTConnect possible. When you are trying to create a revolution, you need people who are close friends with the movers and shakers—that is Paul Warndorf. The challenge in creating a revolution, such as MTConnect, is that you have to attack from all sides—the manufacturers or the end users, the machine tool builders, the manufacturing equipment providers outside the machine tool world, the software companies in manufacturing, board members, CxOs, machinists, government leaders, internal and external politics—in other words, you have to be able to wear multiple hats and influence countless individuals. There are thousands of ways MTConnect could have died, and thanks to Paul it did not.

I am very proud of the work I did with Dave Patterson to plant the initial MTConnect seed and lay out the roadmap for MTConnect. What we laid out in 2006 continues to be the plan today. Of course there are adjustments and additions along the way, but the fundamentals are all still there.

It was AMT that initially funded MTConnect. We used working groups made of industry experts, which was the exact same approach that Sun used to create Java. It worked for Java and it is working for MTConnect. As you can see, we were able to pull together a diverse group of very smart people like Paul Warndorf, John Byrd, Doug Woods, Dr. Dave Dornfeld, Will Sobel, and Dr. Armando Fox, and many others to create these MTConnect working groups.

John Byrd has said that MTConnect will be more important in the 21st century for manufacturing than CNC was for manufacturing in the 20th century. I could not agree more. MTConnect continues to grow at an incredible pace, and I know John Byrd will be proven 100 percent correct.

Turner's Five Laws of Manufacturing

I first met John Turner, director of technology for FA Consulting and Technology (FAC&T), when he was working for GE FANUC and I was at Sun Microsystems. We met at an MTConnect meeting. I was immediately impressed with John's deep and broad knowledge of manufacturing and his ability to take complex concepts and synthesize those into clear, concise, and compelling points. John and I work together on MTConnect as consultants, and we have presented together on a few occasions. I always learn something new from John. John has done a tremendous amount of work on the MTConnect standard. His background is impressive:

- 30+ years of experience including history with GE and GE FANUC Automation
- Specialization in manufacturing process intelligence and systems optimization and a Six Sigma Black Belt
- Broad business experiences as well as product and operations management
- Applications engineering and software systems development
- Member of the AMT Technical Issues Committee and MTConnect Technical Advisory Board

On a number of occasions John and I have discussed that just having a shop embrace MTConnect as the standard, open, and royalty-free protocol as the means to connect the shop floor to applications is not enough. You must have a data-driven manufacturing mindset and a champion. I told John that what we need to do is educate shop owners and plant managers on his own Five Laws of Manufacturing.

These are John Turner's Five Laws of Manufacturing:

1) We measure what goes in to production and what comes out, but we have little data on what really happens on the production floor.

2) Anyone who says, "I know exactly what is happening on my plant floor"—don't believe them.

3) We don't gather data because it is hard, and someone has to look at it.

4) No one solution or set of data works for everyone.

5) If you don't have an avid champion, save your time and money.

John's five laws really are critical points that any shop or plant should discuss before they invest in a shop floor monitoring package.

Law #1 states, "We measure what goes in to production and what comes out, but we have little data on what really happens on the production floor." This law is something that we hear about way too often. This is where a shop or plant has a great deal of data and processes regarding both part design and part inspection, but has a big hole in the middle regarding data on actual part manufacturing. This is analogous to a race car team spending a lot of time and money on the design of the race car and then breaking the car down after the race to see what has held up and what did not, but not gathering data during the actual race. You would never see that scenario in racing, yet we see it all the time in manufacturing.

Law #2 states, "Anyone who says, 'I know exactly what is happening on my plant floor'—don't believe them." Shop owners or plant managers who have been so close to their operations for a long time sometimes can't see issues/opportunities from a new perspective. This is the shop owner or plant manager who is in denial. If they do not have a shop floor monitoring package, they are absolutely kidding themselves. The anecdotal stories in this area are endless. Yet, for years now years, many shop floor software monitoring companies have told me that only one or two percent of shops/plants have a monitoring package.

Law #3 states, "We don't gather data because it is hard, and someone has to look at it." I have a lot of respect for this law because it really drives home two key points. The first part of the first point is about gathering data, and MTConnect can address that. MTConnect is the open and royalty-free protocol that is enabling a universal method of attaching manufacturing equipment on the shop floor to applications. Think of MTConnect as the "Bluetooth of manufacturing." The second part of Law #3 is a real cultural issue that is not obvious to most individuals in manufacturing. There is also an implied message in the "and someone has to look at it" part of John's Law #3. The message is that someone needs to analyze the data, make recommendations on how to fix the issue, deploy the fix, and then monitor that the fix is working as designed. Sometimes those in manufacturing think that a shop floor monitoring package provides answers—it does not. Much like an MRI, it provides data that must be properly interpreted and then acted upon.

Law #4 states, "No one solution or set of data works for everyone." While this law first seems like it is in the common-sense category, you would be amazed at how many shops or plants expect a piece of software to be configured out of the box with the ability to grab the exact data needed, analyze the data, and present it in a format that both management and the machinist on the floor can use. A fundamental question such as, "What are the top five problems you believe you have on the shop floor today?" can generate hours of conversations with a different priority list depending on whom you ask at the shop or plant.

Law #5 states, "If you don't have an avid champion, save your time and money." This might be the most important law of all five. Monitoring for the sake of monitoring will not be successful. Using monitoring as a weapon of mass data on the shop floor is also a great recipe to turn the shop floor against management. The right analogy is one that the military uses. Everyone's job in the military is either to directly or indirectly support the warfighter. The same should be said of the machinists and those on the manufacturing floor. Everything that is being done with shop/plant floor monitoring should be done with those on the shop floor in mind. I like to think of the machinist as the neurosurgeon with shop floor data being the CAT scans, x-rays, and MRIs that help the machinist do his or her job much better. If shop floor monitoring is being used as a stick, then don't bother because both your morale and productivity will go down.

I have become convinced that every time I speak on MTConnect I am going to bring up Turner's Five Laws of Manufacturing. The reason is that the first and obvious application that individuals think of with MTConnect is the acquisition of a shop/plant floor monitoring solution. While most companies that want a floor monitoring solution purchase the application, some companies write their own. This is typically the first step of many for data-driven manufacturing. Once a shop/plant realizes that understanding what is happening on the shop floor can improve overall productivity, they quickly realize the many other areas where this and other data can be integrated to improve all aspects of their business. Of all of Turner's Five Laws of Manufacturing, the most important very well might be having a champion. In my opinion, having a strong champion that can drive change by utilizing shop floor data will be the single most important factor in the success or failure of a shop/plant floor monitoring project.

Whether it is simply monitoring the shop floor or total integration of all your data in manufacturing, I would first strongly encourage a shop or plant to have an open discussion of Turner's Five Laws of Manufacturing with all involved parties.

How Do You Know that Is the Real Problem?

When I was at Sun Microsystems, one of my favorite questions to a new systems engineer would be eight simple words, "How do you know that's the real problem?" This question typically came about as preparation for an upcoming customer visit. The sales team might be bringing me in to discuss Sun's future software and hardware directions under a non-disclosure agreement. The pre-briefing scenario would usually be the sales representative giving me the historical background of the account, how much business they are looking at doing with the customer this year, and the major hot buttons for this particular customer. The systems engineer would then give me the technical overview of the account. The engineer might make a statement such as, "they need new workstations because they cannot run their primary application fast enough." My next question would be, "How do you know that's the real problem?" The response would be, "That's what the customer told me," to which I would respond, "So, you really don't know, but this is what the customer told you." The bottom line would usually be that it was an opinion without any data to back it up.

When I give a talk on MTConnect, I like to ask a few questions. The first question is, "Who here is doing lean manufacturing? Please raise your right hand." I then say, "Ok, put it down. Now, who here is doing Overall Equipment Effectiveness, please raise your hand." I then ask, "If you are doing either lean or OEE, please raise your right hand and keep it up." Then I say the following, "Please also raise your left hand if you are monitoring your shop floor. By shop floor monitoring, I do not mean simply counting good and bad parts, nor do I mean simply knowing what color is on the stack light. By shop floor monitoring, I mean the ability to know anywhere and anytime exactly what a given piece of equipment is doing in your plant or shop. Invariably only a tiny percentage of the left hands are in the air, but over 50 percent of the right hands are up. I then state, "Unless you have both hands in the air, you might think you are doing lean or OEE, but you are not. It is impossible to do either lean manufacturing or OEE if you do not know what is happening on your shop floor and unless you are monitoring your shop floor, you don't know what is really happening on your shop floor. You might think you are doing lean or OEE, but you are just kidding yourself." No one has ever challenged me on that. They don't because it is the truth.

I am a huge believer in science and data. I am extremely leery when someone says that they "think with their gut." Don't get me wrong, I am not saying that the good or bad feeling in your gut cannot augment a decision, but when it is used for more than a very small percentage of decision making, especially in business, you are in trouble. In the purely personal realm, sometimes a gut feeling is all you need to realize a person or a particular situation is trouble. In business, having the data to back up your decision should be the preferred option.

One of my favorite quotes is from Senator Daniel Patrick Moynihan of New York who famously stated, "Everyone is entitled to their own opinion, just not their own set of facts." The primary challenge, with any type of data, is always context. Politicians are great at using numbers without context. A famous quote that implies the importance of context is from President Ronald Reagan who once said about economists, "trust, but verify." That is the right path to take with customers as well. No one would question a customer in the way that I questioned a junior Sun systems engineer, but it is certainly within reason to ask the customer if it would be ok to take a closer look at the situation.

One of best pieces of advice comes from Albert Einstein who said that if he had one hour to save the world he would spend 55 minutes defining the problem and only five minutes finding the solution. This is in-line with the famous quote by Benjamin Franklin, the most brilliant American who ever lived in my biased opinion, "if I had eight hours to cut down a tree, I would spend six of those sharpening my ax." Both of these quotes have to do with allocating the right percentage of your time in dealing with a given situation. How many times have you been in a meeting and someone raises their hand and asks the question, "Can we please define what problem we are really try to solve here?" It is interesting how often there will be a prolonged silence after that question is raised.

Another favorite story of mine involves speaker wire. A good friend of mine was convinced that he had to spend an ungodly amount of money on the T-Rex Super Shielded Mega Mother Speaker Wire for his home theater. I asked him the question that I like to refer to as "Groundwater's Law" after Neil Groundwater, a genius consultant at Sun Microsystems. Groundwater's Law is "How do the little electrons know?" Specifically I asked my friend, "How do the little electrons know that this expensive speaker wire is so much better than unshielded? Has the vendor quantified the difference?" More importantly, I asked him, "Can you tell the difference?" When I offered to bet him $1,000 that he could not tell the difference with his ears, he decided to look into it. He went with unshielded speaker wire and has no regrets.

Let's look at how MTConnect comes into play when a shop owner makes the statement, "I am looking at adding a third shift because we are not currently making our production schedule." A logical question might be, "How do you know that is the real problem?"

This is where MTConnect is elegant in its simplicity. For those of you new to MTConnect, here is a short primer. MTConnect can be thought of as the Rosetta Stone/Bluetooth for software applications. MTConnect is the protocol pipe that connects manufacturing equipment to software applications. For example, you would not go to your electronics store and buy just Bluetooth. Bluetooth comes with your cellphone and your headset. Bluetooth is simply the protocol, or the rules of how these two devices will speak to each other, so you can tie your cellphone to your headset. MTConnect is simply the protocol that connects your manufacturing equipment to your software applications, such as monitoring software, your enterprise resource planning (ERP) system, or any other piece of software. Since MTConnect is an open and royalty free protocol that uses proven Internet standards, it is absolutely brain-dead easy for today's software applications to speak to an MTConnect-enabled piece of manufacturing equipment.

Monitoring applications that will provide real-time data on what is happening on your shop floor using the MTConnect protocol is the first step for any shop owner. The second step is getting that information integrated into that shop owner's entire business. Through MTConnect, you will discover that your real problem was not having the data you needed to make the right business decisions to improve your shop or plant.

Chapter 4: Do You Know More About Your Car than Your Plant or Shop?

Lord Kelvin's Check Engine Light

The National Institute of Standards and Technology (NIST) was my account for six years starting in the mid-1980s at Sun Microsystems. As a systems engineer, I loved having NIST as an account because NIST was always doing something very interesting and pushing the limits on what Sun could provide in terms of computing power. On one of my first visits to NIST, I was brought into a conference room and saw the following engraved in the floor:

"I often say that when you can measure what you are speaking about, and express it in numbers, you know something about it; but when you cannot measure it, when you cannot express it in numbers, your knowledge is of a meager and unsatisfactory kind; it may be the beginning of knowledge, but you have scarcely in your thoughts advanced to the state of Science, whatever the matter may be."

—Lord Kelvin (Sir William Thomson)

This phrase is built into the DNA of computer science and science in general. This phrase really changed my way of thinking. It summarizes the problem with most challenges by asking, "Have you quantified the situation?" To provide a simple example of this, when you walk into a data center that houses thousands of computers in countless racks, you will find that every single one of those computers are monitored extremely closely. Again, let me remind you that only one to two percent of machine tools are monitored today. This percentage is mind-boggling to me. How can any plant possibly make intelligent decisions if they cannot quantify what a machine tool is doing?

Why are only one to two percent of all machine tools being monitored today? It comes down to two reasons—technology and culture. Too often when you speak to someone at a smaller job shop or plant, the reason for not monitoring is the cost and/or time to implement. MTConnect addresses the technical side of the challenge by making it is easy to get data off a machine tool in an open, royalty-free, and standard fashion. MTConnect's mantra is "Different Devices, Common Connection." Doug Woods created that phrase and it is brilliant. When I first started consulting at AMT, I told the story of Java and the slogan "Write Once, Run Anywhere™" (WORA). That simple phrase by Sun Microsystems was all that was needed to get the point across regarding the benefits of Java. Sun could have gone on discussing the technical benefits of Java using every buzzword in the computer industry. We could have said that Java is an object-oriented language without the use of pointers that uses an intermediary set of bytecodes that run on top of a virtual machine that gives a level of portability to cellphones, PCs, and mainframe computers in the hopes of limiting the tremendous expense of regression testing by having different source code and binaries for the plethora of computer architectures, platforms, and processors in the industry today. That does not roll of your tongue like "Write Once, Run Anywhere" does it?

Once a month, or whenever I want to login, I can go out to my car's manufacturer and get a detailed report on all of the important systems. This begs the question, "Do You Know More About Your Car Than Your Plant or Shop?" The challenge with manufacturing is that question is unfortunately answered "yes." Under no scenario can this make any sense. Think about this, you are sitting at home and you can easily find out exactly what is the status of all your systems on your car, but it is impossible to find out what is going on right now with your shop or plant without picking up the phone and calling someone? This is insane!

MTConnect is all about dramatically lowering the entry barrier to enable a machine tool to speak to the rest of the world in an open fashion with the first and most obvious application being monitoring your shop or plant floor. MTConnect can address the technical side of this challenge, but how do you change the culture component of this equation? As we all know, culture is a huge issue when driving change. This is true whether it is in a business or any other activity that involves humans. Education is the key to driving culture changes, and there are many educational lessons from the computer industry that can be applied to manufacturing to help drive this needed culture change.

Metcalfe's Law

Let's look at some of the laws in the computer industry and see if there are similarities in manufacturing. Bob Metcalfe, the inventor of Ethernet, made a statement that has now become known as "Metcalfe's Law." Metcalfe's Law basically states that the value of any network is the number of users or devices connected to the network squared. If we apply Metcalfe's Law to manufacturing, we would modify it slightly to state: The value of any manufacturing shop floor's network is the number of pieces of manufacturing equipment that can speak MTConnect squared. Why MTConnect squared and not just the number of pieces of manufacturing equipment squared? Because it is MTConnect that makes these pieces of manufacturing able to all speak the language of the Internet, which is XML. XML is an abbreviation for eXtensible Markup Language and it is the default Internet language today. By speaking the language of the Internet, it makes it extremely easy for software applications to talk to MTConnect-enabled manufacturing equipment.

Everything You Know Is Wrong and Scaling is Always the Problem

Two of the most brilliant people I know are Neil Groundwater and Mike O'Dell. I am fortunate to call both of them my friends. When I was hired as a systems engineer at Sun Microsystems in early 1987, Neil was the consultant in the office. The technical buck stopped with Neil at the Sun Tysons, Virginia, office. When the systems engineers had a very difficult question, we would walk over to Neil's office. Neil had an office—we had cubes. We all knew our places in the IQ food chain. Neil chose his parents well. Unlike some very technical individuals, Neil also has a great personality and is someone you can talk to. There are many extremely technical and gifted individuals who are devoid of any social skills whatsoever; this is not Neil. One of the phrases that Neil told me about, which is one of my favorite phrases of all time is "Everything You Know Is Wrong." As Wikipedia points out, *Everything You Know Is Wrong* is the eighth comedy album by the Firesign Theatre released in October 1974 on Columbia Records. I have used the phrase for a number of talks, videos, webinars, and presentations. Neil introduced me to Mike O'Dell.

Mike is a Venture Partner at New Enterprise Associates (NEA). Below are just some of the points that are brought out at NEA on his extremely impressive experience and interests.

- His primary interest is the structure and behavioral dynamics of large, complex systems.

- Mike came from UUNET Technologies where he was chief scientist, responsible for network and product architecture during the emergence of the commercial Internet.

- Prior to UUNET, Mike held positions at Bellcore (now Telcordia), a GaAs SPARC supercomputer startup, and a U.S. Government contractor.

- In the halcyon days of the ARPAnet, he was "liaison" for IMP-34 at Lawrence Berkeley Laboratory and spearheaded the transition from NCP to TCP/IP at the Department of Energy National Laboratories.

- Mike served for four years as area director for operations and management in the IETF, authored several IDs and RFCs, and helped birth RADIUS and SNMPv3.

- He was founding editor of Computing Systems, an international, refereed scholarly journal.

I had the privilege of going on a week-long vacation on the Intracoastal Waterway with Mike and Neil on Mike's super yacht. Here is the URL if you want to see pictures of the trip. http://tinyurl.com/NeilMikeDave. Mike has a very unique way to turn a phrase. I remember one day on Mike's yacht there were some issues with the engines and Mike said, "A boat is a series of horrendous choices." Another phrase he used was "Why use lead when gold will do?" This is a popular phrase at Lawrence Berkeley National Labs in Berkeley, California. It must be nice to have that type of budget.

On the trip we talked about a lot of things, and my favorite was hearing real-life examples of "O'Dell's Law" of computing.

O'Dell's Law, as I love to share with people, is made up of two key components:

1. Scaling is always the problem.

2. If you are not afraid, you simply do not understand.

These are beyond brilliant. These are like the $E=MC^2$ of computing. When you are designing any type of software system, it is easy to design to run with a small number of people, a small number of devices, or with a small amount of data. Take the same software and tell the developers that the requirements were off by five orders of magnitude. You were slightly off in the number of users. It was not 15 users; it was 1.5 million users. Ask them if they will need to change anything about their design. Simply put, scaling is **always** the problem. The other issue is the unknown. Software has so many moving parts that it takes just one small, "gee, I forgot about that," to break everything. It is always interesting to hear folks who are not in software say, "I don't understand why this no longer works," when a new release comes out or "Why does software take so long to write?" Because to do it right, you have to hire really smart people with lots of experience; give them clear guidelines; the tools to design the software; and the time to get it all done, tested, and out the door. A non-trivial process.

A very old engineering saying that is one of my all-time favorites is *"Fast, good, or cheap. Pick any two. You can't have all three. Not with carbon-based units."* I added the carbon based units parts since we know this is true with humans on planet Earth. I have used this quote so often at AMT that people quote it before I have a chance to state it. Fast, good, or cheap is the mantra of great consultants. Good consultants answer clients' questions and great consultants question clients' answers. That is an old adage as well. This is like the speed of light, it is not just a good idea, it's the law.

One of the most common misconceptions about MTConnect is that it is an application that you purchase. MTConnect is a standard and a key part of that standard is the protocol that defines how manufacturing equipment will speak to the outside world, as well as a dictionary of what these manufacturing terms mean. Think of MTConnect as Bluetooth for manufacturing with a dictionary of terms. Why do I emphasize the dictionary? It is the dictionary that gives meaning to the manufacturing terms. For example, imagine the English language without a dictionary. What would we have? We would have 26 letters and words without meaning. Without a dictionary of words, we would have everyone defining their own words and that is exactly what we had with manufacturing prior to MTConnect.

Former Secretary of Defense Donald Rumsfeld liked to say, "there are known knowns, known unknowns, and unknown unknowns." Stated another way, "you don't know what you don't know." The real purpose of MTConnect is to quantify the known unknowns and provide the framework to discover the unknown unknowns. You cannot manage what you don't know. And unless you are quantifying what you don't know, then you are shooting from the hip, which is never a good idea.

So, why would Lord Kelvin *love* MTConnect? Because in order to quantify how well a manufacturing plant or job shop is doing, you first must easily get the data and put it in a standard quantified form. That is exactly what MTConnect does. Getting the data in an open and royalty-free way is what will allow you to first monitor what you are doing and then to share the information with all your applications and all your partners. While the most obvious use of getting common information out of a piece of manufacturing equipment is monitoring, that is just the tip of the iceberg. The real win with MTConnect is when quantified information is available anytime, anywhere, to any application, to any partner (in a secure fashion), and on any device it drives productivity up. I would imagine Lord Kelvin would change MTConnect's mantra to be, "MTConnect— to measure is to know."

Tear Down Those Stack Lights!

We have all seen the check engine light come on a car we have been driving. More times than not, it is because someone did not properly put the gas cap on tight enough. However, there are times when it is more serious, and sometimes it is extremely serious. The check engine light is also sometimes called an "idiot light," because it comes on and provides no real concrete information. Typically, the check engine light is amber. If it comes up in a red color, you are likely in a world of engine trouble. The check engine light is just an indicator of a problem. It comes on when the system determines a problem. In manufacturing, the check engine light is typically the stack light. If the operator can control the stack light, then that makes about as much sense as having a toggle switch on your dash for the driver of the car to turn on the engine light when he or she thinks or knows there is some type of problem. Think about that for a second. There is absolutely no difference between having the driver turn on a toggle switch and an operator of a machine tool turn a stack light from green to yellow or red. If the stack light is supposed to be an indicator of what is really going on with that particular machine tool, for all practical purposes your manufacturing check engine light is broken. So what do you do about it?

Just as President Ronald Reagan said at the Brandenburg Gate on June 12, 1987, "Mr. Gorbachev, tear down this wall!" As president and chairman of the board for the MTConnect Institute, I am saying to manufacturing shops and plants around the globe, "Manufacturing plants and shops tear down these stack lights!" The wall that separated East Germany from West Germany kept people and ideas apart. The stack lights in plants are just as dated, remind me of the Cold War. These stack lights are keeping real information from reaching those who need to know it. When I walk into a plant and see stack lights I always just roll me eyes thinking to myself, "What year is this anyway 1913 or 2013?"

Many drivers do not realize that on every car made since 1996, there is a connector or port that is typically right below the steering wheel. This port is called the On-Board Diagnostics

II port or OBD-II. What is very important about the OBD-II is that it is the same physical connector and same protocol (how you speak to the OBD-II electronically) for all cars. This means that if your check engine light comes on, instead of just tightening the gas cap and hoping the light goes off after a few cold starts, you now have the ability to find out what is really going on. There are OBD-II scanners on the market that allow you to plug in to the OBD-II port to find out in much more detail exactly what is going on with your engine. These typically go from $70 to $200 if you want to buy one, or many times you can borrow one from your local auto parts store. How these work is that you plug them in, turn on your car, and you are able to retrieve information from the OBD-II. Many of these scanners allow you to capture data while your car is running. After driving your car, you can then download this information to your computer for further analysis or replay what your engine did while you were driving. What these scanners can do varies by the price, but typically the first test users will run is scanning for codes. Scanning for codes means going through each of the subsystems of your car looking for error codes that might have been set. The scanners do not tell what to fix, but they typically narrow it down significantly to the areas where you should be looking. What is the OBD-II for manufacturing? MTConnect is the virtual OBD-II port for manufacturing.

MTConnect is an open and royalty-free standard for manufacturing that is connecting manufacturing equipment with applications by using proven Internet protocols. Again, I ask you to think of MTConnect as the "Bluetooth for manufacturing." With Bluetooth, both devices must speak Bluetooth for anything useful to happen. Just as simply having an OBD-II port on your car does not provide you with any more data unless you have an OBD-II scanner, the same "pairing" principle applies to MTConnect and software applications. You can have an MTConnect-enabled machine tool or piece of manufacturing equipment, but without the software to read and analyze the data you do not have both sides of the equation. The OBD-II scanner is really the application or the tool that you use to help you understand what is happening with your engine. In manufacturing, it is software applications, such as shop floor monitoring systems that speak to an MTConnect-enabled piece of manufacturing equipment.

Remember what Lord Kelvin said, the first "essential step" to learning any subject is to measure it and "express it in numbers."

ABS: Ability to Brake and Steer in Manufacturing

ABS stands for Antilock Braking System. This tells us a definition; it does not completely convey how ABS helps a driver in terms of capabilities. Before we explore ABS and relate it back to manufacturing, it might be helpful to put this technology into historical context.

If you are old like me, born during the Eisenhower administration, then you probably have memories of your father taking you out in your 1960s or early 1970s vintage Family Truckster during the winter to learn how brake in the snow. Your dad probably took you to an open school parking lot, during a snow day, for a lesson. Your father would get the car up to 25 mph and then slam on the brakes. You would slip and slide, eventually ending sideways or doing a 360. He then would repeat the exercise, this time pumping the brakes. This would usually bring the vehicle to a stop in a straight line.

Then it was your turn. After you did the usual 180° or 360° spinouts after jamming on the brakes, then it was your turn to try pumping the brakes to see the difference. While doing the pumping exercise, your dad would typically be yelling in your ear like wild man, "Pump the brakes, pump the brakes!" Then your father would summarize that now you knew what to do in a panic stop in the snow.

Fast forward to 2013. Today's father takes their kids out, tells them the story I just shared with you as they go to the school parking lot. The big difference now is that that father just tells the kids to slam on the brakes as hard as they can and bring it to a stop in a straight line. The ABS system comes into play by pulsating many times per second at each wheel to keep traction and bring the car to a stop safely. Here is the problem: with most fathers that is the entire lesson, just stand on the brakes and let the car bring you to a stop, but they are missing half of the equation.

We know what ABS stands for but what does it allow the driver to do? ABS could also mean "Ability to Brake and Steer." It allows driver to do both at the same time. The reason this is so important is that many times the person in front of you has done something stupid in the snow, and simply stopping might not be the best course of action. Braking and steering around that car might be the best course of action. Another example is if a pedestrian walks out in front of you and there is simply no time to stop. In this scenario, braking and steering around the pedestrian in the snow is the best maneuver.

We see this ABS scenario today in manufacturing with MTConnect. I have mentioned before that today on planet Earth, only one to two percent of machine tools are monitored and that this small percentage comes down to two reasons—technical and cultural. Too often when you speak to someone at a smaller job shop or plant, the reason for not monitoring is the cost and/or time to implement. MTConnect addresses the technical side of the challenge by making it easy to get data off a machine tool in an open, royalty-free, and standard fashion. MTConnect's motto is "Different Devices, Common Connection." MTConnect is all about dramatically lowering the barrier to entry, enabling a machine tool to speak to the rest of the world in an open fashion.

At the first ever MTConnect: Connecting Manufacturing Conference ([MC]²) in November of 2011, there were exhibitors showing off both software and hardware solutions to enable both small plants and large shops to easily monitor their manufacturing equipment in a cost-effective manner. We are seeing dramatic cost changes in lowering the barrier to entry to attach a very wide variety of manufacturing equipment using MTConnect. A number of solution providers are offering small black boxes, the size of a brick, which attach to legacy manufacturing equipment on one side and enable MTConnect via Ethernet or Wi-Fi on the other side.

Monitoring your shop is a great first step, because in order to quantify how well a manufacturing plant or job shop is doing, you first must easily get the data and put it in a standard quantified form. That is exactly what MTConnect does. Getting the data in an open and royalty-free way is what will allow you to first monitor what you are doing and then to share the information with all of your applications and all your partners.

Let's remember what MTConnect is and is not. As mentioned before, one of the most common misconceptions about MTConnect is that it is an application that you purchase. MTConnect is a protocol that defines how manufacturing equipment will speak to the outside world as well as dictionary of what these manufacturing terms mean. Again, think of MTConnect as Bluetooth for manufacturing with a dictionary of terms. Without a dictionary of words, everyone would be defining their own words. That is exactly what we had with manufacturing prior to MTConnect.

Remember, MTConnect can be thought of as the Rosetta Stone for software applications. Your software applications speak to a piece of manufacturing equipment using the MTConnect protocol, and valuable information about the capabilities and what specifically that manufacturing equipment is doing comes back to your applications. Your applications do not need to learn all the specifics of each different piece of manufacturing equipment out there. Your software applications use MTConnect as that Rosetta Stone for getting information. This makes a huge difference in terms of integrating your plant floor with your data center and the rest of the world.

While the most obvious use of getting common information out of a piece of equipment is monitoring, that is just the first half of the equation. Monitoring your shop or plant is the equivalent of the ability to brake with ABS. But that is not the entire equation. The real win with MTConnect is the ability to steer your company with the information that MTConnect is providing. When this quantified information is available anytime, anywhere, to any application, to any partner, and on any device, you are steering your business, and that is what truly drives up productivity.

Let's recap a few things. If you are teaching your kids how to drive in the snow, tell them ABS stands for Antilock Brake System, but what it gives the driver is the Ability to Brake and Steer. When you take them out, tell them that you want to press firmly on the brakes, but then have them also steer to get out of trouble if they need to. Remind them to work with technology and take advantage of everything that ABS gives you and not just settle for half of the equation. It might make a big difference someday.

The same principle applies to MTConnect. The first half of MTConnect equation is getting an application that will monitor your shop or plant floor using the MTConnect protocol. The second and most important half is getting that information integrated into your entire business.

Shops that have implemented MTConnect have told me that the difference between how they were operating in the past and now after they have implemented MTConnect is the same analogy as trying to stop in the snow in a big old 1966

Buick Electra 225 vs. a brand new 2013 SUV with ABS. With the old Buick you were just glad if it stopped without hitting something. With the new vehicles you can reliably brake and steer your way clear of trouble in a predictable fashion. Think of MTConnect as the enabling technology that allows software applications to deal with the challenges ahead and the ability to steer your business to greater productivity.

Chapter 5: Manufacturing in the Cloud

If you Google "cloud computing," you will get about 105 million hits. That is a lot of hits for any topic, but that is certainly a lot for a topic that most folks have difficulty defining. The reason for this is not that it is a complicated topic; the reason is that cloud computing is an umbrella term that has multiple definitions. If you ask 10 people what the term cloud computing means, you're likely to get 10 different answers. Flickr, Gmail, Google, LinkedIn, Facebook, QuickBooks, SalesForce.com, Carbonite, and Farmville are just some examples of applications that run in the cloud.

Cloud computing has the potential to be game-changing technology in manufacturing for everyone from small shops to extremely large manufacturing plants. The key is understanding the process, asking the right questions, and making wise provider decisions.

Big Data

"Big data" is the latest terminology for dealing with the age-old problem of too much data that cannot be handled with the known popular tools of the time. Twenty years ago the term for big data was High Performance Computing or HPC. Sun Microsystems did quite well in the HPC market before cloud computing came along. Then Sun started losing to the racks and racks of Linux boxes that were all "good enough." Admiral Grace Hopper was another innovative mind who could clearly predict the path ahead for technology, including how to deal with big data.

Admiral Grace Hopper, the lady who supposedly defined the term "computer bug," created COBOL (COmmon Business

Oriented Language) and has made many impressive contributions to the world of computing. As the Naval History and Heritage Command reports, "Moth found trapped between points at Relay #70, Panel F, of the Mark II Aiken Relay Calculator while it was being tested at Harvard University, 9 September 1947. The operators affixed the moth to the computer log, with the entry: "First actual case of bug being found." They put out the word that they had "debugged" the machine. In 1988, the log, with the moth still taped by the entry, was in the Naval Surface Warfare Center Computer Museum at Dahlgren, Virginia."

Admiral Hopper was prophetic when she stated on the prospect of building bigger and bigger mainframe computers, "In pioneer days they used oxen for heavy pulling, and when one ox couldn't budge a log, they didn't try to grow a larger ox. We shouldn't be trying for bigger computers, but for more systems of computers." This is really what happened and what cloud computing is all about. For those of you old enough, there is a good example of what Admiral Hopper is referring to. Back in the 1980s and 1990s, when someone purchased a new PC, they would always state the clock speed of the CPU. For example, "I just bought a 750 MHz Dell computer." When Gordon Moore of Intel stated, "The number of transistors incorporated in a chip will approximately double every 24 months" and this became famously known as "Moore's Law," it turns out Grace Hopper was right. We don't have 14GHz processors, we have processors that have an increasing number of cores inside of them and this, along with high bandwidth is the foundation for cloud computing.

Cloud Computing

At the International Manufacturing Technology Show (IMTS) 2010, the Emerging Technology Center (ETC) featured a cloud computing area that was a big hit. I am proud to say that I designed the cloud computing area for the ETC. A typical conversation about cloud computing, in order to explain the term, went like this.

"When you Google something, do you know specifically what city the servers are located in where your search query is actually being run? For that matter, do you care?"

The answers were usually something like, "I don't know and I don't care. I simply want my results to come back to me quickly."

Then I would ask, "Would you rather have a small nuclear power plant in your backyard that you owned and managed, or would you rather just pay for what you use from the electric company?"

The answers were, as expected, "I just want to pay for the electricity that I use and not worry about it."

That is exactly what cloud computing is all about at a high level. From a technical standpoint, large server farms are used that someone else runs and maintains (loading new software, upgrades, patches, virus protection, and so on), the user pays for exactly what is used, and in return they get their requested results.

Cloud computing is important for manufacturing because it allows companies to avoid the countless lists of business and technical issues associated with running their own data centers and to save money by only paying for the computing resources when they need it on a "pay-as-you-go" model.

To truly understand and appreciate the benefits of cloud computing, it is important to first understand the key building blocks—fast bandwidth, the Web browser, and large server farms.

Fast Bandwidth. Instead of moving the data equivalent to a paragraph per second during the dark days of dial-up, you can now move a book per second with broadband. With these huge communication pipes, the planet just got a whole lot smaller.

Web Browser. Sometimes it is easy to forget how ubiquitous the browser is for software applications for both home and office.

Large Server Farms. There are hundreds of thousands of computers that are heavily used during a couple months each year, but then just twiddle their processor bits the rest of the year. Amazon is the classic example. The company is very busy during November and December, selling books and goods, but the rest of the year, the systems are lightly used. Someone at Amazon came up with the brilliant idea of selling time on those systems to offset the huge costs of running hundreds of thousands of computers.

With these three technical pillars of cloud computing in place, it allows software companies to offer their software on these large server farms as a "service." In other words, users simply point their browser at the software in the cloud and off they go. Users pay for what they use, when they use it.

Why are software companies rapidly moving more and more of their applications to cloud computing? Because users are demanding it and are tired of running their own "nuclear power plants." They are tired of buying lots of servers and then learning that these servers are only being used on an industry average of eight to 15 percent of the time. Users are tired of all the patching, upgrading, malware, viruses, and the plethora of issues that come along with running their own data center. This is especially important for a small manufacturing shop, where there's no time to constantly worry about all of the patches, upgrades, and system administration work.

SalesForce.com is a classic example of cloud computing. Many credit SalesForce.com with starting cloud computing by offering Customer Relationship Management (CRM) as a Software as a Service (SaaS). SaaS is one of the categories of cloud computing that most manufacturing companies are interested in using. SaaS took SalesForce from a long and detailed list of what servers a customer needs to support a large CRM system onsite, to a simple and straightforward, "All you need is a browser and you have a CRM system." SalesForce.com takes care of the rest. This is only one example of the dramatic differences between cloud computing and the standard method.

Pay by the Drink

The most important part of cloud computing is the elasticity of the cloud for businesses. Elasticity means the ability to scale up (add computers dynamically) and scale down according to business needs. SalesForce.com worries about having all the processing power and storage available for their customers. The beauty of cloud computing from a customer's viewpoint is as you need more or less computing power or storage, it is simply turned on or off in the cloud.

Scalability applies to large, global manufacturing companies as well. Let's say a company is using software in the cloud for one of its manufacturing plants and the president says, "This is working out well—let's use this for all of our plants worldwide." At this point, the company informs the cloud computing software company of this new need and the number of computers in the cloud will be made available as the new plants start using the software. In contrast, the traditional model would call for months of sizing exercises to determine how many new servers would be needed for each plant and purchasing and then configuring the software at each of these plants. With cloud technology, the other plants can be enabled in minutes instead of months.

MTConnect is an example of the importance of cloud computing in manufacturing today. MTConnect is an open and royalty-free protocol standard that allows manufacturing equipment to have a common language to exchange information. As machine tools start spitting out gigabytes of information per hour, it doesn't make sense to store all this information locally. Even for a large manufacturing plant, no one wants to invest in a lot of servers that will be antiques in less than four years. However, it makes the most sense to securely store this information in the cloud and use as many (or as few) processors to analyze this data as needed while paying only for what is used. John Meyer of IBM, likes to show a slide of big data where the largest amount of data comes from sensors. MTConnect sensors will be a tremendous growth area in the next five years.

Beware the Roach Motel

There are important checklist items to verify when selecting a company that has a cloud version of its software or a cloud provider that will be the development platform. At the top of this list is proper security. The University of California, Berkeley, white paper, "Above the Clouds: A Berkeley View of Cloud Computing," written by U.C. Berkeley's Reliable Adaptive Distributed Systems Laboratory, offers a lot of valuable information for considering cloud computing.[13] Topics include data confidentiality and audit-ability, data lock-in, data transfer bottlenecks, availability of service, and performance unpredictability.

The first two topics deal with security. The level of security is totally dependent on the level of security the cloud provider has in place. Security is an end-to-end problem. Whether dealing with a small manufacturing shop or a large global manufacturer, it is critical to ask clarifying questions to understand the security that is being provided. The first two questions to ask a cloud-computing vendor are: "Is my data secure at rest?" and "Is my data secure in flight?" You are asking whether your data is encrypted on their storage devices and as it is being moved from one point to another. If the answer is anything but an unequivocal yes, then raise the red flag. Start with these questions, but they are certainly not the only security questions.

Now it is important to understand if your cloud provider is a roach motel in terms of data storage. How easy is it to get data out of the cloud? This answer becomes important if the cloud computing company were to go out of business and take the user's data with it.

After addressing security concerns, the next issue is the availability and performance of the cloud computing provider. It is important to have the Service Level Agreement (SLA) in writing. The SLA defines the percentage of uptime the cloud provider guarantees. If the cloud provider does not state a number in a contract, make sure to receive a credit for the time the provider was down. SLAs do not guarantee recouping the loss of business revenue for downtime. So, it is critical to understand the specifics of an SLA and have a contingency plan in place for times the service is down.

In addition to SaaS, there are two other categories of cloud computing: PaaS or Platform as a Service and IaaS or Infrastructure as a Service. PaaS and IaaS are for companies that are developing their own software. PaaS provides components that allow developers to combine these components or "mash up" to create new applications. IaaS provides the ability to create virtual machine images (VMI) and run these VMIs in the cloud. All software companies should investigate SaaS, PaaS, and IaaS.

Here are three things to ask software vendors about cloud computing and specifically SaaS:

- Do they have a cloud version of your software? If they do, you need to understand all the pricing options. Also, understand the ability to migrate from a cloud version to a standard software version in the future, if you choose to do this down the road.

- Security, security, security. You must understand all the issues here.

- Performance and availability. Get it in writing and understand the issues.

Cloud computing should be investigated, whether you are a small manufacturing shop or a large global manufacturer. If you are a software company in manufacturing, then you don't have a minute to waste before investigating cloud computing because your customers will be demanding it and it is the logical next step in a product road map. But, as with any technology, it is important to separate the quality cloud providers from the disreputable cloud providers.

I wrote an article for *MoldMaking Technology Magazine* in the fall of 2011 and was sent a number of questions from astute readers who each had a number of well-thought comments regarding concern about a lack of control. Their concerns are likely the same as your concerns. I have addressed them as follows.

"Access to data/software depends on a working Internet connection (connection goes down, work flow is interrupted for those cloud services)."

This is absolutely true if all of your services run in the cloud. The obvious questions that need to be quantified are "What percentage of time was your Internet provider down last year?", "Did it affect your production?", and "Was it simply an inconvenience or did business stop?" Those companies that rely on an Internet connection typically take the necessary steps to pay their Internet service provider (ISP) for a SLA that guarantees a certain level of uptime, or they have alternate plans in place.

"Software upgrades are at vendor's discretion, not the end-user's."

It depends what type of cloud computing we are talking about here. If we are discussing the most popular type of cloud computing—SaaS—then that statement is absolutely true. I would argue that this is a feature and not a bug. As a business, you don't want to take on handling your own software patches and upgrades. You should be focusing on your business instead. In most cases, SaaS patching and upgrading is much, much more professional than your typical end-user's IT department.

"Data could be compromised, outside of our internal control."

This is true if your data is not always encrypted. Your data should **always** be encrypted whether or not it is in flight or at rest. In flight means your data is being moved over the network. At rest means when the data is on a storage device such as a disk drive. This could also be true if there are poor security procedures in place at the cloud-computing provider.

"Vendor lock-in with your data could occur (i.e., no way to move your data from one cloud supplier to another)."

This is an important concern and the reader makes a great point. This is called the "roach motel" of cloud computing. The roach motel analogy means your data checks in, but you can never check it out to move it someplace else. This is so important that you should have it stated it writing how, when, and in what format you can retrieve your data from the cloud provider. An example of this would be a SaaS enterprise resource planning (ERP) offering with no ability to export all of your data so you could never switch ERP providers. Scott McNealy, Sun Microsystems president and CEO, first coined the phrase "Total Cost to Exit" (TCE) in the early 1990s. TCE is about the ability to move/migrate both software and the data to other hardware and software vendors. TCE is something everyone who is considering cloud computing needs to ask their potential software providers.

"I am familiar with cloud computing, but we do not use it due to potential security leaks, etc. With a company our size and the amount of sensitive information we have, we keep very tight reins on IT security/information storage and transfer. I'm sure as (cloud computing) becomes more mainstream, more companies will turn to it. Like anything else, as soon as this service proves to be a definite, safe, cost-effective way to store, use, or transfer knowledge, everyone will migrate to it. Right now it is very confusing."

Security is far and away the No. 1 concern that users express regarding cloud computing. The underlying reasons are obvious. "If the data is not in my data center, then how do I know it is safe?" My answer is, "Do you do online banking?" In other words, the level of security is totally dependent on the level of security the cloud provider has in place. Security is an end-to-end problem. Is your local system secure? Is your network secure? Is your data secure on your cloud provider? Security must come first when you are investigating cloud computing.

"I've heard some talk of it [cloud computing], but have not seen implementation at any tool suppliers or molders I work with. "

This is an area where we are slowly starting to see manufacturing in general embrace cloud computing. The economics for cloud computing make so much sense from a business standpoint that it is not a matter of "if" for most companies, it is a matter of "when." But, let's be clear that there are applications that do not lend themselves to the cloud. Applications that require real-time controls are examples of ones that do not work well in the cloud.

I write and have recorded videos on the topic of cloud computing. If you want to learn more, I would suggest you visit my blog at http://photonsandelectrons.blogspot.com/ and watch the three cloud computing videos that I put together with AMT (http://tinyurl.com/DavesCloudVideos).

Whether or not you have plans to investigate cloud computing, at a minimum, you should ask your software providers what their cloud computing plans are. If your software provider has no such plans, that should set off a number of alarms in your head. If your software provider does have a cloud-computing plan, you should learn the business and technical advantages of their plan. Ask the big questions first: "How does this save me time and/or make me money?" The advantages of cloud computing are real and cloud computing is here to stay. But, just like any technology, the right answer to the question, "Does this make sense for me?" is "It depends." Take time for an in-depth discussion of your current situation and where cloud computing might make business sense. It's worth a close investigation.

Chapter 6: Monitoring Systems to Manufacturing Intelligence

Who Watches the Watchmen?

"*Quis custodiet ipsos custodes*" is approximately translated to "Who will guard the guards?" As manufacturing becomes more and more about software, the importance of monitoring your computer networks will increase significantly. By computer networks I am referring to all of your systems that are not specifically manufacturing equipment. The ability to absolutely know that your software is up and running well becomes imperative.

Back in the late 1980s there was a huge rush of companies that came out with network monitoring programs. Companies realized they were investing significant sums in their servers, PCs, Macs, workstations, routers, bridges, and networks so they needed to monitor and maintain these expensive and important resources. Sun Microsystems was an early leader with a product called SunNet Manager. It was a great product that used graphics and the ability to drill down and send alerts to keep everyone updated on a real-time basis

There were two big challenges with network management and these were not technical, but a combination of cultural and business challenges. They were so prevalent that I would start my SunNet Manager presentations with this statement, "I am going to ask you two questions. To the first question you will give me the answer 'everything,' and that will be the wrong answer. The second question you will respond with, 'I don't know,' and that will be the right answer."

The first question was, "What do you want to monitor?" I would then explain that with hundreds of metrics, monitoring everything is not viable. The next question from the customer would be, "Well, what do you suggest then?" That would usually receive a high-level answer, "It depends, but certainly there are important metrics for any system in terms of CPU load, network load, disk drive access, memory usage, and types of applications running to name just a few." While this answer was technically accurate, it really did not address their question. For example, many times monitoring software would be used as a foundation for a high availability class of systems. High availability systems are those systems that typically require four nines or 99.99 percent or greater uptime. This means a total downtime of less than one hour per year. However, just because a high availability system is up, does that mean that the database is running properly and accepting transactions? Just because a computer is running and all the processes appear when you issue a process status command, it does not mean it is operating properly end to end.

The second question I would ask was a very tough one. "What do you want to *do* when, through your monitoring efforts, you discover an event?" This is the human side of monitoring the monitor. That was the really tough question because it would involve both technical and business input. For example, your primary server is running very slow because it is running out of memory, which processes do you want to kill? Not an easy question on a shared server. You can certainly take a look and see if a specific process is out of control, but what happens if this has just been a slow and gradual increasing of load over time and not an obvious out-of-control metric? What if everything is running fine, you just have too many processes for the server? Buying and installing more memory might be an option or even buying another server; however, that does not answer the question, "What do you do right now?" If this happens at 2:30 a.m. on a Saturday night, who makes that decision? Who is monitoring the monitor? Is it software and/or a human? Are all the decisions automated, or is it a workflow that involves humans at a specific point?

There are many common threads between both monitoring your shop floor and your computer network. An important area is one of governance. Governance is simply the definition of the policies that one will follow as well as the enforcement of those policies. Governance and the common threads are why I decided to mention Turner's Five Laws of Manufacturing. Monitoring your shop floor or your computer network is not enough, you must have a culture of being data-driven that is led by a champion. Data-driven manufacturing is where decisions are made with data from a variety of systems in a logical fashion with input from all of the stakeholders. Just as a reminder, below are Turner's Five Laws of Manufacturing.

1) We measure what goes in to production and what comes out, but we have little data on what really happens on the production floor.

2) Anyone who says, "I know exactly what is happening on my plant floor"—don't believe them.

3) We don't gather data because it is hard and someone has to look at it.

4) No one solution or set of data works for everyone.

5) If you don't have an avid champion, save your time and money.

Monitoring your computer network is much easier than monitoring your shop floor because it is a well understood science and there are tons of tools out there in terms of open source and proprietary monitoring software.

It used to be that you had to install the software locally for computer network monitoring. Today, there are numerous cloud monitoring services that will monitor your systems. Very detailed monitoring still typically involves locally installed software. More and more companies are using software in the cloud to substitute or augment software that they previously would load and run locally. Many of these companies in the cloud monitor their own systems and have impressive uptimes. But what happens when these services are down? How do you know? Are you notified? What actions can you take when a vital cloud service your business depends on goes down? This is where *"quis custodiet ipsos custodes"* or "who watches the watchman" comes into play.

As a company starts to put monitoring in place, it is very helpful to remember the "Eight Fallacies of Distributed Computing" by Peter Deutsch that James Gosling points out on James' blog. Peter and James both worked at Sun Microsystems.

1. The network is reliable.
2. Latency is zero.
3. Bandwidth is infinite.
4. The network is secure.
5. Topology doesn't change.
6. There is one administrator.
7. Transport cost is zero.
8. The network is homogeneous.

The main point of the above list is to never assume the condition of your network when developing software or monitoring systems—you must know.

Whether or not you are monitoring your shop floor or computer network, there is no "insert here" canned-magic solution in terms of what is important to monitor. And there is no script explaining what should be done when events occur. What is most important is putting together a team led by a champion to evaluate the data, take action, monitor your actions, and continue to adjust. This team should be made up of a variety of disciplines and must meet on a regular basis.

As you introduce monitoring into your shop floor and your network, remember Turner's Five Laws of Manufacturing and the Eight Fallacies of Distributed Computing. Finally, your goal in monitoring is the ability to answer these five simple monitoring questions:

1. Who will be our monitoring champion?
2. Who will be on our monitoring team?
3. What should we monitor?
4. What will we do when these events occur?
5. Who monitors the monitor?

Whatever monitoring software you decide to go with, make sure you can try before you buy. This is critical. The bottom line is that you can't manage what you can't monitor, and make sure you know what and who is watching the watchmen—*quis custodiet ipsos custodes.*

In a World Without Fences, Who Needs Gates?

This phrase appears on my all-time favorite Java One t-shirt that I still wear to this day. I am talking about sales strategies. "Give away the razor and sell em' the blades." We have all heard and seen this type of sales strategy. The standard model is to come up with a proprietary product, separate the consumables, and make your money selling the consumables. Specifically, sell the main product at a greatly reduced price and then lock them in forever on your proprietary consumables.

We see this type of sales model in all types of businesses. It is not uncommon to see this scenario in the computer industry and manufacturing. This razor/blade scenario in software ends up being much more expensive for the customer in the long run. How software vendors do this is very slick because of the sales story that gets wrapped around it. If you do not take the time to think through the lifecycle of your software purchase, you can easily fall into this trap. Here's how to avoid it.

I have had this discussion more than a few times lately and the conversation usually starts off with two questions on monitoring their shop or plant floor such as, "Dave, why should I care how I get my data? All I care about is the information I see on my monitor that tells me how my machine tools are running." My response is, "You're right, you shouldn't care, unless you think your shop will change or you plan on using the data coming off those machine tools in something besides monitoring."

The software sales rep typically responds with, "Don't worry about it, it's just a black box" when the shop/plant owner asks how the software will connect to the manufacturing equipment. The conversation might end at that point and the customer goes ahead and buys the software.

At this point, the software sales rep knows they have locked the customer in when changes at the shop or plant occur. As we all know, changes always happen in business. The scenario unfolds as follows. The customer calls up the sales rep and says, "We just purchased a new machine tool and I would like to connect it up to my monitoring software. What do we need to do in order to make that happen?" The sales rep then has two responses. Either they have the adapter for the new machine tool or they don't. If they do, then there is usually a charge for the adapter as well as charge for someone to come out from the software company to install it. If they don't have it, then they will offer to have someone from their professional services organization price writing the adapter. This is typically someone who will cost you $150 to $250 an hour to write that adapter. If you decide that you want to integrate the monitoring software with other software in your existing enterprise, then you will likely be charged to have this type of integration work done as well.

The price can be high, so it is natural to think about different ways that you might be able to get the adapter written for less money. "Get a consultant" naturally jumps to mind! You reach out to a few consultants and they all tell you the same story. The software company does not document how to write adapters or how to integrate with their software. You are locked in to the vendor. You are now in what I like to call Adapter Hell. This Adapter Hell is why only one to two percent of all machine tools are monitored today.

Adapter Hell is why it absolutely does matter how the adapters speak to the manufacturing equipment. Would it be different if you had an open and royalty free, as well as open source, type of protocol for the adapters such as MTConnect? MTConnect speaks in the exact same language that runs on the Internet today—http and XML. The beauty of http is that it is the same protocol moving information around that you also see in your browser bar when you type in http://ESPN.com. XML is the data language of the Internet. In other words, it is the letters, words, and dictionary that describe the data itself. Here's the bottom line with MTConnect—it gives you freedom. It gives you the freedom to have someone else besides the software vendor provide the adapters for you.

Instead of being in Adapter Hell, by using MTConnect you end up in Adapter Heaven. Since MTConnect is open source and based on standards, it is easy to find someone to write an adapter. You are not locked in to the vendor. Again, since MTConnect is based on XML, it is brain-dead easy to integrate that information into your other software.

So, does it matter *how* you get the data? It depends. Would you rather go to Adapter Heaven or Adapter Hell? Gates are what some software vendors want to put up so they can charge you outrageous prices for adapters as well as very expensive installations of those adapters. That is why in a world without proprietary fences, who needs software adapter gates? How do you avoid Adapter Hell? The next time a software sales rep tries to tell you, "it's just a black box, don't worry about it," make sure you ask that person how they are getting the data and make sure that software vendor has MTConnect as an option. Adapter Heaven is much better place than Adapter Hell.

83% of Radiologists Were Blind

Let's imagine that you are a world-class radiologist. To give you some concept of what it took for you to reach this point and where you are today, let's assume the following:

- You graduated top in your high school
- Spent four years at a university to complete your under grad
- Four more years in medical school
- Three years of residency
- You accumulated $350,000 in school debt by the time you graduated
- You have 20 years of experience in a practice
- You make $450,000 a year in salary

Your job is to examine this CT scan looking for anything unusual.

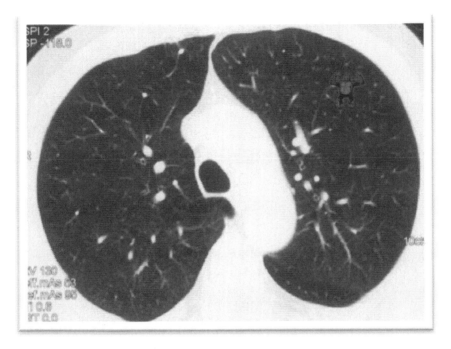

Figure 4. *A scan very similar to the image above was shown to 24 radiologists in a recent study. The image is of a pair of lungs.*

Trafton Drew, Melissa L. H. Vo, and Jeremy M. Wolfe showed an image like Figure 2 to 24 radiologists as part of a recent study that will be published in a forthcoming paper in *Psychological Science.*

[14] What do you, as a world-class radiologist, notice in this CT scan?

Take another look at this CT scan on the next page.

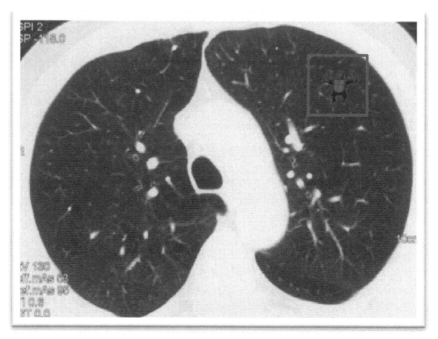

Figure 5. *A gorilla image was hidden in the CT scan.*

In her *Washington Post* article titled, "Study: Most radiologists don't notice a gorilla in a CT scan," Sarah Kliff reported, "Trafton Drew, Melissa L. H. Vo, and Jeremy M. Wolfe **had 24 radiologists look** at **CT scans of lungs**, scanning them for lung nodules, which could be cancerous." The article went on to state, "Eye-tracking revealed that, of the **20 radiologists who did not report the gorilla,** 12 looked directly at the gorilla's location when it was visible."

Here is the amazing point of this article, 83.3% of the radiologists did NOT see the gorilla.

The article went on to ask, "How much does this matter for radiologists?" They are never, after all, going to encounter a gorilla on a real scan from a patient. It does, however, suggest that specialists could easily miss other red flags when they are on the search for one specific indicator. "Why do radiologists sometimes fail to detect such large anomalies? Of course, as is critical in all IB [inattentional blindness] demonstrations, the radiologists were not looking for this unexpected stimulus," they write. Even experts "operating in their domain of expertise, are vulnerable to inattentional blindness."

Wikipedia defines inattentional blindness, as the following, "also known as perceptual blindness, is failure to notice an unexpected stimulus that is in one's eyesight when other attention-demanding tasks are being performed."[15]

What about non-experts? Kliff stated, "On the more positive side, the radiologists did perform better than the untrained eye: When the researchers ran a group of non-doctors through the experiment, no one noticed the gorilla on the scan."

How does this relate back to manufacturing and shop floor monitoring? It must be true that 98 to 99 percent of all manufacturers believe they are the world-class neurologists for their given industry because they believe they can see and know everything that is going on by just walking around the plant. They don't know. They are blind.

Cradle to Grave—All Corvettes Are Red

One of my all-time favorite books is by the author James Schefter and titled, *All Corvettes Are Red.* The book came out on January 1, 1998. This book is considered an all-time classic in the Corvette crowd. What is fascinating about this book is that the author was given unlimited access during an eight-year time period where he could literally be a fly on the wall and sit in on any meeting he wanted to that involved the Corvette. Schefter had access to anything at GM provided he told no one besides his wife while he was working on the book. The book is extremely well written and provides a never-before, behind-the-scenes look at product development. I read this book when a good friend of mine and a Corvette expert, Steve Ferry, asked me what I thought about the new C5 (5th generation Corvette that came out in 1998). I told Steve that I like how Corvettes looked, I liked how they accelerated, but I was not a fan of the build quality and some of the ergonomics of Corvettes. Steve just said, "go read *All Corvettes Are Red*." I did and it completely changed my mind on Corvettes. What changed my mind was the amount and quality of the engineering, testing, and monitoring that GM put into the Corvette. I now own two: a black 1998 Corvette with 430 hp and a 2011 cyber-gray metallic Grand Sport Corvette with 445 hp. With my wife's Mini Cooper S convertible, we have well over 1,000 hp of cars in our garage. I told my wife that a 1,000 hp of cars in one's garage is the key for a successful marriage. We have been happily married for almost 30 years so it must be true.

What do Corvettes, MTConnect, and monitoring have to do with each other? Most people who own cars have received a recall notice in the mail before. Usually these recall notices are for a particular vehicle over a range of years. These recalls can be extremely expensive for automobile manufacturers. For the sake of an example, let's create a hypothetical situation that in February of 2014 GM is getting complaints on the new LT1 V8 engine that is in its new Corvette Stingray 2014 model. Specifically, the complaint is excessive use of oil. The new LT1 engine is consuming a quart of oil every 350 miles, which is (again hypothetical) three to five times what should be expected. What does GM do? They start gathering the data to discover if it is a design problem that is causing this issue or is this just an anomaly of the 22 that have been reported so far? With the introduction of this new C7 Corvette Stingray (C7 is the seventh generation) GM wants to protect its reputation at all costs, so the reaction must be correct. GM does not want to panic and recall all of the Corvette Stingrays, nor do they want to appear to be hiding a legitimate problem. The stakes are clearly quite high. Management wants as much data as possible to make the decision.

What we are seeing more and more from the larger manufacturers is the desire and sometimes the requirement that suppliers provide detailed information on each part. This level of information is many times called "cradle-to-grave" part tracking. Cradle-to-grave tracking is absolutely going to become the norm and not the exception in upcoming years. Let's go back to the Quality Assurance (QA) and Engineering Departments for Corvette and the data that they would like to provide management so that the correct decision could be made.

If GM had required standardization with MTConnect for its manufacturing and its suppliers, then the process would take on a very scientific and data-driven approach enabling GM engineers to take a very detailed look at the problem. First, they could pull the serial numbers of the LT1 engines from the Vehicle Identification Number (VIN). Using this data from those LT1 engines, they could then drill down into the specifics regarding the parts that could affect an engine burning too much oil. They could drill down into the suppliers of the engine block, the head, the pistons, the piston rings, the head gasket, the valves, and any other parts that could possibly contribute to this situation. They could go to their suppliers and state, "we want all the MTConnect data from the machine tools that made the following parts" and list those. By examining their Enterprise Resource Planning (ERP) systems, GM could determine which parts were put into which engines and from which suppliers. By using the MTConnect data from each part in that range, GM would run analytics to determine the common characteristics of the engines that have been reported to be using too much oil.

Lord Kelvin's phrase that you have seen me use in this book again and again can be summarized, "you can't manage what you cannot measure." This becomes especially important in troubleshooting whether or not you have a manufacturing problem or a design problem. In either case it must be addressed. In the hypothetical Corvette Stingray situation, the problem was the oil control ring from a particular supplier in Trenton, Illinois, where the MTConnect data reported that they sent GM a batch of these out-of-spec rings on August 24, 2013. By having MTConnect and all the supplier data in MTConnect form, GM was only forced to call 114 owners of the new Corvette Stingray to offer them a replacement LT1 engine. This was tens of millions of dollars less expensive than having to recall the 8,091 Corvette Stingrays that had been delivered up to that point. The 114 owners were pleased to get new engines and GM received great press because it had the data to act appropriately.

The ability to track a part and its MTConnect data, from cradle to grave will be a game changer for manufacturing. Again folks, I made this example up to drive home a point, there is nothing wrong, that I know of, with the new Corvette Stingray. I plan on buying one in the not too distant future, just don't tell my wife.

It is worth retelling the story of the name of *All Corvettes Are Red*.[16] Schefter is sitting in a late night meeting where the entire Corvette team is discussing the quality of paint and the colors that should be on the new Corvette. The test race drivers for Corvette were even in this meeting. Finally, John Heinricy, a very famous racer, stated, "Why are we even having this discussion? All Corvettes are red. The rest are mistakes." Schefter wrote that down and that became the name of his all-time classic book. If you see a red Corvette with the custom tags ACAR it is not saying "this is a car," but rather it is an abbreviation and a tribute to James Schefter's book.

6.241×10^{18} Electrons

The formula above is a coulomb, or the number of electrons that pass a given point in one second, which constitutes one ampere. A volt is defined as the difference of potential that would carry one ampere of current against one ohm resistance. The kilowatt-hour is a unit of energy equivalent to one thousand watts of power expended for one hour of time. Manufacturing uses lots and lots of kilowatts and those costs can be significant.

I like Wikipedia's definition of the smart grid which is, "an electrical grid that uses information and communications technology to gather and act on information, such as information about the behaviors of suppliers and consumers, in an automated fashion to improve the efficiency, reliability, economics, and sustainability of the production and distribution of electricity."[17] That definition touches on all the important areas with economics being a very important component of that definition. Without the right economics and ease of getting information, the smart grid will be a nice-sounding buzzword.

The challenges connecting the factory floor to the smart grid can be described as a three-legged stool. One leg is the ability to easily get information from the smart grid. Another is the ability to easily get data from manufacturing equipment and devices. The third leg is the ability to easily enable commercial software applications to speak to the smart grid and to manufacturing equipment while providing the information needed for manufacturing to make the necessary adjustments to reduce their electrical costs.

It is important to contrast the image that most people have of the smart grid with what is needed for manufacturing. Most individual's image of the smart grid is that of their local power company installing a number of control devices to their A/C compressors, refrigerators, and other power-hungry home equipment with the intent of turning these devices off for short periods of time during peak loads. These devices intercept power while allowing the electrical company the ability to turn these devices off for short periods of time without significant negative effects. By allowing this, homeowners save on their monthly bill, and the power company can deal with the peak-load demands in a more effective manner. Building a new power plant is much more expensive than properly managing what you have. This vision of the power company controlling what gets turned off and when is simply not viable for manufacturing, as no manufacturer would ever allow the electrical company to turn off power when it is producing parts. The question then becomes, what is the right vision and framework for manufacturing to embrace the smart grid?

The Department of Energy (DOE) lists five fundamental technologies that will drive the smart grid. Two of those five are important for this conversation:

- Integrated communications connecting components to open architecture for real-time information and control allowing every part of the grid to both "talk" and "listen"

- Sensing and measurement technologies to support faster and more accurate responses such as remote monitoring, time-of-use pricing, and demand-side management

These two fundamental technologies are also key components to manufacturing. These are also important tenants of the MTConnect protocol in providing an easy-to-use mechanism for manufacturing. It is important to note that much, but not all, of what is needed for this effort is already in the MTConnect standard.

There is a lot of work that needs to be done. It would be helpful to have a standard smart grid interface where the software developer could simply "probe" the smart grid to determine what types of information are available. In this way, there would be a universal mechanism to speak to the variety of electrical companies out there in a standard way. This is exactly how MTConnect treats manufacturing equipment and this model scales well. By using data collected to maximize manufacturing equipment use and based on energy prioritization, overall production costs can be quantified so decisions could be made to lower electrical costs. To provide this enhanced capability, developments are required from various new enabling technologies providing common data acquisition and analysis capabilities at the individual process level, as well as new applications and computational capabilities. The implementers of the smart grid should consider the MTConnect model when they are creating their own standard and universal Application Programming Interface (API) to speak and listen to grid communications. I was on a smart grid panel at the International Manufacturing Technology Show (IMTS) 2012 and was told by an electrical industry representative that some power companies are providing web interfaces, which is an important step in the right direction.

There are a number of shop floor monitoring software companies that are offering devices that are used to monitor the power usage of a given piece of manufacturing.

A typical hardware solution might support MTConnect compatibility in legacy devices and sensors that do not have native MTConnect support. Many of these devices support data collection over serial, analog, and digital interfaces to offer a variety of factory equipment. It is not unusual for these devices to come with a power meter for energy and power quality monitoring, which can be applied along with optional sensor inputs in monitoring the activities of the machine tool. There are a few that enable wireless data transfer and integration by using state-of-the-art mesh networking. I have Z-Wave set up at my house and it has been very reliable, but then again I am not sitting in a manufacturing plant with lots of photons flying around.

The important enablers of the smart grid with MTConnect will be about making it easy to get information from the many power companies around the globe so manufacturers can take action to save money by adjusting their peak-load activities to other times. A great example of this was a study that TechSolve did showing that by having a manufacturer simply run their air compressors at night, the manufacturing plant could demonstrate real cost savings by reducing the need for the air compressors to run as often during the day.

What is at the forefront of a plant manager's mind, when it comes to electrical costs? Peak-load pricing. Peak-load pricing is the higher rate business pay for electricity during given time frames. If a manufacturer can monitor their peak load and move parts manufacturing to other shifts to avoid moving up to the next pricing tier, it could be the difference between a profitable and non-profitable day.

SmartGrid.gov states the following on their website, "The U.S. Department of Energy's (DOE) Office of Electricity Delivery and Energy Reliability has partnered with local utility companies to host Smart Grid Peer-to-Peer Workshops throughout the country. These meetings provide vital support to smart grid implementers who are working to overcome challenges and make the Smart Grid a reality."[18] At the MTConnect Institute, we have had conversations with DOE, power companies, and national labs regarding MTConnect and the smart grid. Hopefully, the United States will decide to make serious infrastructure investments to make the smart grid a reality, which will help manufacturing and all Americans. Unfortunately, with the current state of politics, there is little hope for significant investments in this area at the Federal level in my opinion.

MT*Insight:* Manufacturing Business Intelligence

The blog, *Manufacturing Executive* asked the following question, "What technology would manufacturing managers  use in their future factories?"[19] It was interesting because the answer was "Manufacturing managers identified one clear-cut winner: manufacturing intelligence software. Sixty-nine percent of respondents indicated that they would employ MI software five to 10 years from now; 49 percent do so today." As Wayne Gretzky said so well, a good hockey player plays where the puck is; a great hockey player plays where the puck is going to be. Manufacturing Intelligence, or MI, is where the manufacturing puck is going. There is the data that comes off the shop floor that goes to the numerous MTConnect-enabled shop floor software companies. This software provides a clear view of what is happening on the plant or shop floor. But what about the rest of the plant? What about taking the shop floor monitoring software and integrating it in with the rest of the plant? How about where the manufacturer fits in their respective industry?

I wear a few hats when I consult and one of them is working with the brilliant folks at AMT to help them build what I strongly believe is the best manufacturing business intelligence platform called MT*Insight*. MT*Insight* is a business intelligence website operated by the AMT -- The Association For Manufacturing Technology. I bring up MT*Insight* because once a manufacturer gets their shop or plant floor enabled with MTConnect and starts monitoring their shop floor, then what? The answer to that question is integration into the rest of the manufacturing enterprise.

It is important to point out that MT*Insight* is a platform for a number of apps. What is a platform? A platform is the architecture or foundation where the applications run.

Everything with MT*Insight* runs in the cloud. MT*Insight* is not one app, but it is the platform that houses many apps and that list is growing all the time. Here is a snapshot of the apps as of March 2013.

There are a number of very exciting apps at MT*Insight* such as:

- Laser Systems Product Report
- Sell Your Products
- IMTS 2012
- Thread Rolling Report
- Map U.S. Markets
- MT News
- U.S. Foreign Trade Report
- Cutting Tool Product Group
- Advanced Work Holding
- U.S. Manufacturing Technology Orders (USMTO)

Some of the apps listed above are only available for those who participate in given surveys or other criteria that is listed at MT*Insight.*

First, an explanation of what is manufacturing business intelligence. In the case of MT*Insight,* manufacturing business intelligence is a triple entendre. What is a triple entendre? A triple entendre is a phrase that can be understood in any of three ways, such as in the cover of the 1981 Rush album *Moving Pictures.* If you look at the album cover you will see some people dressed in red that are a moving company carrying some paintings out of the building, some of the people are crying or emotionally moved and there is also a movie crew moving a "moving picture." Three different uses of the "moving" concept. I thought it was important in a manufacturing and open systems technology book to have a reference to the classic rock group Rush. Side note—if you ever see Rush at Lisner Auditorium at George Washington University and are 10 rows back front and center, bring ear plugs. That is not theoretical advice. Manufacturing business intelligence is one of the phrases used to describe MT*Insight,* now let's examine its triple entendre.

- MANUFACTURING Business Intelligence

  - AMT has an incredible amount of manufacturing data that they have collected, are collecting, and are paying to use as well as the many sources of free data on the Internet data. This definition is really about creating or manufacturing business intelligence. This data is incredibly rich and very important for the users of MT*Insight.*

- Manufacturing Business INTELLIGENCE

  - This definition is that platform that includes the many applications are all part of MT*Insight.* MT*Insight* has many applications that all provide intelligence for manufacturing businesses.

- MANUFACTURING BUSINESS Intelligence

  - This definition is about all of the expertise and data that AMT has for the MT*Insight* platform. By platform I mean all of the many applications that make up the MT*Insight* family.

Being the person who created the phrase "Manufacturing Business Intelligence" on November 24, 2010, I hoped that those three words would be as clear, meaningful, and easy to understand as the phrases "Write Once, Run Anywhere" for Java and "Different Devices, Common Connection" for MTConnect. You say those four words and people instantly get it. My 78-year-old mother gets it. Unfortunately, manufacturing business intelligence might have been too clever by half. The challenge is explaining what business intelligence means.

Business intelligence (BI) can be thought of as a three interconnected components. Below is what you want in your BI company.

1. You want as many adapters and connectors as possible to talk to the countless varieties of data sources out there from databases, to websites, to proprietary formats that come in every bizarre format under the sun, to screen scraping software, to CSV files, to Excel files, to open office formats, to binary files, to log files, to you name it. The key is provide a company tons of adapters.

2. Second is the analytics. You want a company that can slice and dice the information in countless ways. I like Wikipedia's paragraph on BI: "BI technologies provide historical, current, and predictive views of business operations. Common functions of business intelligence technologies are reporting, online analytical processing, analytics, data mining, process mining, complex event processing, business performance management, benchmarking, text mining, predictive analytics, and prescriptive analytics."[20]

3. Third is the ability to view a variety of dynamic reports and dashboards on every device that you can think of from your browser on your desktop to your Android™ device and everything in between.

Now that we have defined manufacturing business intelligence and business intelligence in general, let's look at making decisions with data.

When the 2012 election is reviewed from a statistical standpoint, it will be recognized as the year Nate Silver beat Karl Rove. First, for those who worry that this is a political rant, I have voted Republican, Democrat, and Independent for president since 1980. This is about the importance of data and not about politics. Nate Silver is very famous as an innovative and brilliant statistician in baseball and poll predictions. Karl Rove needs no introduction. I met Karl Rove once on a flight from Colorado Springs to Washington, DC. I could not have more impressed in how smart and how nice he was. You can see Karl and me here on my blog at http://tinyurl.com/DaveAndKarl.

If you were like me on election night 2012, you flipped around from one station to another to see what was being said. I like the statistical nature of the Electoral College predictions. All of the stations seemed to be basically in sync in terms of predicting states. If you happened to see a state go for a particular party, you could turn to a different station and likely see another station call it in a similar fashion. If you were watching Fox News like I happened to be at the time, you witnessed an interesting situation of Karl Rove questioning the Fox News number crunchers' assessment that president Obama had won Ohio. Mr. Rove said it was "early" and "premature" for Fox News to call Ohio for Obama. The anchor Megyn Kelly walked down to the experts and they calmly and rationally explained their math. These experts then were brought back to the set and explained the rational directly to Karl Rove. What came through was the importance of taking emotion out of data analysis.

Just in case you have never heard of Nate Silver, he first became famous as a statistician who used data and metrics to predict how baseball players and teams would perform in the future. In 2008, his FiveThirtyEight blog correctly predicted 49 of 50 states for president, and in 2012 he went 51 for 51 (all 50 states plus the District of Columbia). What is fascinating about Nate Silver is that he comes across as a very calm, smart statistician who takes the many polls that are out there and makes extremely accurate predictions. There is no emotion and it reminds me of the classic line from the black and white

TV show *Dragnet*, where the catchphrase was, "Just the facts, ma'am." Many articles have been written since the election where the basic theme was, "Is punditry dead and has data analysis taken its place?" I will show my bias here in that I prefer data geeks to pundits of any party.

This is where I think of MTConnect. MTConnect is really about providing "just the facts." MTConnect is the open and royalty-free standard that provides "just the facts" coming from manufacturing equipment. This data typically ends up in shop floor monitoring dashboards first with the next logical step being integration into manufacturing systems followed by customers and then the supply chain.

If the 2012 elections were the tipping point for data over pundits, then I believe 2013 will be the year where manufacturing business intelligence will reach a tipping point. All too often we hear why a manufacturing shop or plant does things a certain way and it is typically a statement such as, "that's how dad and grandpa did it." Think about the questions that Nate Silver might ask if he showed up at your plant, shop, or company and wanted to improve productivity. What would Nate Silver want to know first? He would want the truth, no emotion, and "just the facts."

A killer app is defined as an application that is so innovative that it creates its own category. It sells itself because it becomes an "absolutely must-have." I believe that MT*Insight* IMTS was and is a killer app. Many manufacturing companies exhibit at the International Manufacturing Show (IMTS). If you were an IMTS exhibitor and did not look into what this app could offer you, then you missed out on the opportunity to go from having a good IMTS to having a great IMTS. No matter the size of your booth, you should have absolutely invested in the MT*Insight* IMTS App because it was the best bang for the buck for IMTS. The good news is that it is still available for those IMTS 2012 exhibitors today enabling them to still take advantage of post-IMTS sales opportunities.

In my experience, the No. 1 killer app from 1970s through today is VisiCalc, which I was demonstrating and selling back in the late 1970s. I was going to college at night, programming in assembler during the day for the Bureau of Economic Analysis (BEA), and working weekends selling TRS-80s for Radio Shack.

Why was I selling TRS-80s on weekends? First, it was fun and I really enjoyed it. The monetary answer was also pretty good. In 1978 a good friend of mine made $83,000 selling TRS-80s. Today, $83,000 is a very nice income level, but in 1978 that was a whole lot of money to be making per year. If we were to calculate what $83,000 would be equivalent to in 2013 dollars it would be $286,000 per year. When VisiCalc came out in 1979, my friend's income doubled. VisiCalc had changed everything to what would be the equivalent of $572,000, in 2013 dollars, for my friend. Needless to say he was knocking it out of the park. He was the Michael Jordan for Radio Shack computer sales. I was not nearly as good as he was, but I did ok myself. I was making more on a weekend selling TRS-80s than I was during the entire week programming for BEA. Plus, I was having a hell of a lot more fun. This experience helped shaped my thinking on the importance of not only being able to program, but if you can also talk technology and convince people of its benefits, you will pay more in taxes than government programmers make in a year. Life is all about choices and priorities. I certainly took the road less traveled and as they say, that has made all the difference.

A typical demonstration for VisiCalc followed a common scenario. I would sit a customer down, explain the physical components of a TRS-80 and jump into showing off VisiCalc. I would create a very simple spreadsheet and then start adding to it. At some point the customer would say, "Can you do this?"

Then the suggestions would become more and more specific until finally the customer would say, "get out of the chair, I want to try this." At that point I knew I had a sale. At my very best, I probably had a 35 percent close ratio on someone buying a system the first time they saw it. If they came back the second time to see it again, I probably had a 65 percent close ratio. I had an 80 percent close ratio if it was just selling VisiCalc to a user who already had a TRS-80.

MT*Insight*'s IMTS was a killer app because nine out of 10 exhibitors who receive a demo from AMT's Steve Lesnewich, Mark Kennedy, or Kim Brown buy the IMTS app. Let me repeat that number in case you thought it was a typo—a 90 percent close ratio! Certainly Steve, Mark, and Kim are fantastic at what they do, but I would also suggest that it is the tremendous value of MT*Insight* IMTS app that is very, very compelling.

It is interesting to me that the manufacturing industry believes so strongly that trade shows are the best way to sell. I think a lot of this goes back to the great job that AMT has done with the mother of all trade shows and that is IMTS which happens the second week of September in even numbered years. In 2012, the MTConnect booth and the MT*Insight* booth were side-by-side in the Emerging Technology Center (ETC). Both of these booths could have been labeled Manufacturing Intelligence.

I mentioned just how popular the MT*Insight* IMTS app is and if you're wondering why nine out of 10 exhibitors that see a demo of the IMTS app then make a purchase, here are a few reasons that Mark and Kim shared. Reasons to purchase the IMTS app include unlimited access to sell and market to previous IMTS contacts; it invites your previous leads back to your boot;, adds your custom-filtered prospects to your CRM today; provides unlimited access to sell and market to IMTS registrants; and filters prospects by geography, industry, product interest, buying role, job function, and plant size enabling you to find your key customers.

It also targets your marketing campaigns, sends leads to your sales teams and distributors now, sees what days your key customers are coming to IMTS, markets the special events in your booth to visitors attending that day, and finds out when the executives and engineers will be at IMTS. Use the IMTS app to compare your booth performance to other exhibitors in your pavilion, quadrant, building, and the whole show.

Examine your booth traffic and identify new opportunities such as knowing everyone who missed your booth in previous IMTS shows. You can then sell to your opportunities all year long; pinpoint visitor traffic trends to amplify your booth's productivity; help staff your booth with daily and hourly traffic analysis from previous IMTS shows, plan your booth events to maximize floor traffic and effectiveness; visualize never-before-seen data using state-of-the-art interactive tools; create custom reports anytime, anyplace; and export what you need in Excel, PowerPoint, Word, PDF, HTML, and CSV files.

Each of those were individually great reasons to buy the IMTS app, but here's the primary reason why I think MT*Insight* IMTS was and is a killer app. If we were to ask every exhibitor at IMTS what they expected to get out of the show, it would be first sales and then leads. If you look at what sales are all about, it comes down to having the opportunity to show your product and/or service to a qualified customer. The MT*Insight* IMTS app helps you find qualified leads before, during, and after IMTS.

Don't just take just my word for it; here is what Peter Eelman, AMT vice president of exhibitions and communications says: "MT*Insight* IMTS is the type of app that can pay for itself many times over—with just one extra sale. I would encourage all IMTS exhibitors to check out this app at MTInsight.org. We designed this app to help IMTS exhibitors have their best year ever at IMTS." Also, Tom Snyder, AMT's exhibitions sales manager, thinks this is an app that can make a huge difference for IMTS exhibitors. "I've been at AMT for 27 years and working with IMTS exhibitors for 22 years. I can think of no better investment for a successful IMTS than the MT*Insight* IMTS app."

I know that the future for MT*Insight* is very bright, not only for future IMTS apps, such as IMTS 2014, but for **all** of the many apps that make up the MT*Insight* platform.

How has MT*Insight* done? Below is a press release on November 3, 2011, that speaks for itself.

SAN FRANCISCO—(EON: Enhanced Online News)—ActuateOne Live!—Actuate Corporation (NASDAQ:BIRT), The people behind BIRT® and the leading open source Business Intelligence (BI) vendor, today announced that it has recognized AMT—The Association For Manufacturing Technology—with a 2011 Excellence Award in the BIRT Implementation category.

*Overall, MT*Insight *powered by BIRT onDemand enables our members to resolve their own questions, saving them a huge amount of time and money. With the ability to quickly access and analyze huge data repositories, MT*Insight *is a game-changing application for the manufacturing industry.*

*AMT won in the BIRT Implementation category by contracting with Actuate to create MT*Insight, *the state-of-the-art business intelligence platform that runs on BIRT onDemand. In teaming up with Actuate on this project, AMT was able to incorporate the entire body of knowledge into one BI application to allow its users to interact with the data in an easy to use and understandable visual format. With BIRT, AMT's MT*Insight *has become the premier stop for market data, trends and intelligence in the manufacturing landscape, increasing their credibility and keeping them at the forefront of the technology sector.*

"BIRT onDemand provides AMT and its members with a unique plug-and-play platform. Our team required a solution that could eliminate server management costs and reduce IT involvement, as well as integrating BIRT natively into popular mobile platforms for our large base of end users. The flexibility in delivery model really provided an edge over its competitors," says Douglas K. Woods, President, AMT. *"Overall, MTInsight powered by BIRT onDemand enables our members to resolve their own questions, saving them a huge amount of time and money. With the ability to quickly access and analyze huge data repositories, MTInsight is a game-changing application for the manufacturing industry."*

"AMT was able to leverage BIRT onDemand to create the most interactive and usable BI platform for their industry," said Nobby Akiha, Senior Vice President, Marketing, Actuate. "MTInsight demonstrates how Actuate and BIRT can help achieve excellence in a short timeframe, assisting AMT's efforts in helping to spread these best practices within the manufacturing industry."

I realize this sounds like an advertisement for MT*Insight* inside a book on MTConnect and technology, but it is not. This is about the next step after you have easily connected your shop or plant floor with MTConnect—using data to drive more sales if you are on the selling side of manufacturing. AMT runs MT*Insight* in the cloud and for all practical reasons, this gives MT*Insight* unlimited storage and unlimited number of processors. What does the future hold for MT*Insight?* Go to http://MTInsight.org to learn more today! OK, so maybe it was a little bit of a commercial, but you can tell that I am very proud of MT*Insight* and have really enjoyed working with the individuals that have put this together. Manufacturing business intelligence is the logical next step after shop floor monitoring.

Chapter 7: Most Important Invention Since CNC

Mark Albert's Game Changer and Success Stories

The front cover for the December 2009 issue of *Modern Machine Shop* read: "Manufacturing Game-Changer, MTConnect." This article, written by Mark Albert, marked a very important moment in MTConnect's history because it was Mark's article that really put MTConnect on the global manufacturing map and sparked conversations throughout manufacturing.

Over the years, Mark has written a number of articles, blogs, and interviews on MTConnect and has shared his many insights on MTConnect and its effects. Mark wrote in this December 2009 article, "The key 'enabling technology' to be used and tested in this pilot project, initiated in June 2009, was MTConnect (mtconnect.org), a standardized communications protocol designed to make it easier to collect, transmit, and leverage data from discrete equipment such as CNC machine tools. 'We suspected there was a gap between our machining process plans and our machining results. Closing those gaps in our shops and cells would significantly improve machine utilization and reduce both maintenance downtime and manufacturing cost,' says Jim Dolle, who manages the Metal Working & Manufacturing Technology engineering group headquartered at GE Aviation's Evendale facility in Cincinnati, Ohio."[21]

At the end of the day, the only thing companies care about regarding any technology is will it save them time or money or better yet, will it make them money. MTConnect is a means to an end and it is not an end in itself.

As listed at MTConnect.org, according to GE Aviation's Roy Peterson, "Right away, this data gives us a more complete picture of how the machines were performing." Remmele Engineering's Bill Blomquist said, "If a machine is idle or a transfer station is falling behind, we will be better able to find the reason."

"A noteworthy point regarding alarms was made by Stephen Luckowski, Chief of Materials, Manufacturing & Prototype Technology with the U.S. Army ARDEC at the 2011 MTConnect conference: "Typically when the machine alarms, it's too late, the tool is already broken. That means that just collecting and reporting alarms is only part of the problem. To prevent alarms that relate to downtime, we need to use MTConnect to understand the alarm and develop a pattern of what causes the downtime."

We Thought We Knew—We Only Knew 10 Percent

I had the privilege of speaking at the Mori-Seiki Innovation Days in 2011. I was asked by Dana Super of Mori-Seiki to work with one of their top customers, and I was thrilled to do so. It is always better when you can speak to a crowd with someone who has actually implemented the technology. Dana gave me the name of Stewart McMillan of Task Force Tips (TFT). TFT and Stewart McMillan are well known and respected in manufacturing as well as in the computer industry. I shot Stewart and email and we setup a time to speak on the phone.

I called Stewart and he explained to me what TFT does, which is provide first responders with what they need, such as fire fighting equipment, and they are known for their nozzles. It was fascinating to learn all about TFT. One of the points Stewart brought out was that he gave AutoCAD the famous fire nozzle for them to include with their software. For those of you not familiar with TFT's fire nozzle, there were two main benchmarks back in the late 1980s and early 1990s with AutoCAD. The first was how quickly your system could render the Cathedral and the second was the fire nozzle. Both of these were vector drawings of enough complexity to put a strain on the average processor. The time in seconds told you something about the overall performance of the microprocessor and graphics processor on the computer where you were running AutoCAD. The other interesting part of that conversation was when Stewart said to me, "Dave, I first started using Unix on a TRS-80 Model II from Radio Shack in the early 1980s when it ran Microsoft's Xenix operating system." To which I responded, "No you didn't Stewart." I could tell he was taken back on this when he asked, "What do you mean I didn't, I certainly did." I then told Stewart, "That's impossible Stewart and here's why. The TRS-80 Model II was a Z-80A processor that only ran TRS-DOS. In order to run Xenix you would have had to upgrade the Z-80A board up to the 68010 microprocessor by Motorola and upgrade the memory up to 512KB (this is kilobytes and not megabytes of RAM) as well." There's a pause and I hear from Stewart, "You're right, I did upgrade." I then replied, "Do you know how I know that? I used to run a Radio Shack Computer Center and I specialized in selling Xenix systems going back to 1981." We both had a good laugh on that one.

At Mori-Seiki Innovation Days, I spoke for 25 minutes on MTConnect and then Stewart spoke. Stewart is a great speaker and has a tremendous ability to drive home the facts and key points. One of the stories he related to the standing-room-only audience was when he was preparing for our joint talk. He mentioned that he wanted to have some current photos of his plants in his presentation so he grabbed his camera and started to walk through one of his plants taking photos. He saw a young machinist working on a machine tool and noticed that the work-holding device was taking 15 to 20 seconds to grab and hold the part. Stewart knew that it should only take about a half of second when they first purchased that work-holding device about eight years ago. He asked the young machinist "What is going on?" He was told that this device had been acting that way for many months and the young machinist was told that it was a bad pump and when the pump went, then it would be replaced. Stewart then went to the manager of the machinist to ask what was going on. He heard a similar story. Stewart then went to the plant manager. The plant manager said it had been going on for about nine months. Stewart told the plant manager to get a service person out there to look at it. A few days later, Stewart, the plant manager, the manager, and the machinist all are there when the service technician shows up. The service technician looks at the work-holding device, goes into his bag, pulls out a new filter, pops the new filter in and it goes back to its sub-second performance. Stewart calmly explains to the plant manager and manager that he is not upset about the time that has been wasted on this particular machine tool because of this, nor is he upset with the additional cost that was needlessly incurred, what he was upset about was the message it sent to the young machinist. The message was, "if you bring us a problem, we will make a guess on the real problem and not properly diagnose it." Stewart went on to say that if they had MTConnect on that device and were monitoring it, there would have been a variable set so that as soon as the work-holding device was taking 2 seconds to hold the part, that was 100 percent longer than it should take and an alert would go to the appropriate individuals. This is just one simple example, but it drives home the point of "you don't know what you don't know."

Here is a quote from Stewart's talk: "We thought we knew what was happening on our shop floor better than anybody. MTConnect has opened our eyes that maybe we knew 10 percent... It's invaluable for seeing patterns with not just machines but also the operators running them, to watch how often they're adjusting their offsets. It's allowed us to coach our operators to help them get the most out of the machines they run."

TFT is a world-class organization that is a huge supporter of MTConnect and is truly a state-of-the-art company. Huge thanks to Stewart, Nate Price, and the entire TFT organization.

Will Sobel, MTConnect chief architect and president of System Insights, told me that it is not unusual for companies to see a 20 percent improvement in utilization in 90 days and to see a completed return on investment (ROI) in four to six months when implementing shop floor monitoring software where the manufacturing equipment is MTConnect-enabled. This is a no-brainer. Why would a company not want to monitor their shop floor? There are some reasons, but those are all in the category of the shop being very small. Even then, I would argue that there is financial benefit to put in simple shop floor monitoring. They key, as I bring out earlier in the book, is to not get trapped into a proprietary system. Customers should insist on their manufacturing equipment supporting MTConnect in addition to whatever proprietary protocols they might be currently supporting.

In the Hands of Creative Manufacturers and Engineers

Below is a quote that I really like by industry thought leader A.J. Sweatt, of AJ Sweatt Logic and Communications. This statement appeared on his website on January 5, 2009.[22] Mr. Sweatt was very prophetic in this statement on MTConnect:

To say MTConnect is revolutionary is a gross understatement. Connecting machines and collecting data using the same protocol not only gives in-plant management far greater agility and control; it also allows for a level of communications between suppliers, customers, OEMs, sales and international partners that could easily be the greatest achievement for manufacturing since CNC. Or even the Internet itself.

MTConnect is the fledgling, open-source communications standard developed by AMT—The Association for Manufacturing

Technology and Sun Microsystems. Its purpose is to create a consistent communications protocol that connects machines, controls and software in a manufacturing environment to each other, allowing for the management, observation, and control of varied and often disparate units and methods.

An often overlooked element of new technology is discovery. Putting technology in the hands of creative manufacturers and engineers nearly always results in originally unimagined benefits and developments. MTConnect has the potential for great rewards down the pike for two fundamental reasons.

First, it **capitalizes on the power of the Internet** in extraordinarily useful ways, by making it the real-time, data exchange medium it was meant to be. Collecting and sharing part, material, inventory, process, and other data instantly will force manufacturers to develop processes and methods to capitalize on the efficiencies of real-time command and control. Think about creating a seamless network of machines and systems with no borders—a network with nodes that know each other, talk to each other, and know no borders.

Second, MTConnect will offer shops and plants of any size the ability to **connect with markets, customers, and prospects in ways more efficiently than ever before**. For your customers, imagine sharing real-time data with them through a protected extranet that allows them to view progress on their jobs or projects. For prospects via your Web site, think about collecting and publishing specifics about jobs run through your business that portrays your prowess and value as a partner—like improved cycle times, set-up improvements, proficiencies with exotic materials or processes, etc."

Benefits Start Right Away

I had the privilege of visiting Curtiss Wright Controls with Paul Warndorf and Will Sobel. We received a great tour and it is extremely impressive what Gene Summey of Curtis Wright Controls is doing with MTConnect and shop floor monitoring. As you can read in their case study on MTConnect.org, "Curtiss Wright Controls in Shelby, North Carolina, used vimana to improve equipment utilization by over 20 percent in a period of 10 weeks. Curtiss Wright Controls was looking for a solution for manufacturing data collection and analysis with centralized data collection, automatic determination of machine tool utilization, and support for interfacing with different types of manufacturing equipment."[23] The term vimana refers to System Insights shop floor monitoring package.

In the "Getting Started With MTConnect: Shop Floor Monitoring, What's in it for You?" white paper, there is a paragraph regarding MTConnect and energy which states: "Manufacturing is among the most energy-intensive sectors and accounts for almost 30 percent of all greenhouse gas emissions in the United States. Energy consumption monitoring has been done since the industrial revolution days and is traditionally viewed as a 'bill to be paid', which is increasing on an average by 10 percent per annum. There is a wide gap between monitoring energy consumption and actually correlating that data to the operational activities in a factory to devise strategies for energy usage optimization. With the advent of a standard like MTConnect, we can now in real-time 'tag' every kilowatt spent against a particular machine, part, work order, or client. In addition, we have the ability to include infrastructure items like pumps, chillers, air compressors, HVAC, and lighting to provide a holistic view of energy consumption. A manufacturer in the midwest was able to obtain dramatic energy savings by understanding energy usage and demand patterns which enables energy costs to be a controllable operating expense."[24]

Mark Albert, Editor-in-Chief for *Modern Machine Shop*, stated in the February 2013 AMT News the following on MTConnect: "One of the things I'm seeing is that when a company implements it, they start to get benefits right away. Whether they start implementing on a small scale or a larger one, they very quickly start to see rewards that make the effort worthwhile. They start getting a better picture of what's actually happening on their shop floor."[25]

Albert goes on to say in the article, "One of the most immediate examples is machine monitoring, an obvious application for MTConnect. Shop floor managers immediately get greater visibility into activity on the shop floor." It's a great way to monitor efficiency and productivity of certain machines.

But Albert thinks that the future holds much more promise for MTConnect usage. For example, the next frontier could potentially be the ability to monitor energy usage or how much power a given machine consumes. "With the right application, it's going to be easier for companies to actually know what their energy costs are associated with, not just with specific machines, but also specific jobs and specific cutting tools."

MTConnect is not YOUR Secret

One of the challenges with MTConnect is that we have many famous companies that are using MTConnect, but that will not stand up and say so for competitive reasons. They believe MTConnect gives them a competitive edge, and they're correct in that assessment. However, what they do not understand is that they could gain even more of an advantage by shouting from the rooftops that they are using MTConnect because then even more of the machine tool builders, manufacturing equipment providers, and suppliers would start using MTConnect. Would their competition start using MTConnect as well? Maybe, but so what? If these big companies think they can just stand still and not keep innovating, then they are dead men walking anyway and it does not matter. I remember speaking with Red Heitkamp of Remmele Engineering in 2010 on this topic at a conference in Nashville, Tennessee. Red told me, "everyone in manufacturing thinks they have these great secrets." It is counter-intuitive to most in manufacturing that by embracing an open standard and by letting the world know that it will actually make you more competitive. Clearly, the Red Heitkamps and the Remmele Engineerings of the world understand this lesson. Red and Remmele have been huge supporters of MTConnect. I remember at IMTS 2010, a sales rep from a manufacturing company comes up to me and says, "I am looking for Dave Edstrom." I tell him, well you found him. He then tells me, "Red said to come talk to you to understand MTConnect, because if I don't get my company to embrace and support MTConnect, I can kiss any future sales goodbye." I love hearing that.

At the same conference in Nashville in 2010, Red pulled me aside and said something to me that I think about every day as it relates to MTConnect. Red told me, "Dave, it is too expensive and it is too hard for the average shop to use MTConnect. Until you make it easy for the small shop to use MTConnect with what they have on the shop floor today, it will never be successful. At Remmele Engineering we have the resources to pull off MTConnect. Most of the shops are small and that is who you should be focusing your efforts on. When it works for the small shops, it will work for everyone else." Those comments really stuck with me and after the conference I had a call with Red, Mark Conley, and Bill Blomquist of Remmele Engineering to further understand the specifics of what Red was sharing with me. We had a few calls in 2010, and it absolutely resulted in a large number of changes to our plan of attack with MTConnect. There are still challenges that exist in terms of the number of companies that clearly state what MTConnect products they support.

Far and away the number one asked question by those manufacturers that are considering using MTConnect as the common means to get data, "Why can't these MTConnect companies simply list what they support, how much it costs and what I need to do in order to install it?" This is my number one pet peeve as well, if you are going to offer a product that is MTConnect enabled, please take the time to provide your prospects and customers that absolute basic information so they what is supported, how much it costs, and what is needed to be done in order to get it installed. This basic blocking and tackling of marketing and sales would make a huge difference in the uptake of MTConnect *and* the sales of these MTConnect companies.

When I give presentations on MTConnect, I always get questions regarding, "Why would I ever want to monitor my shop floor?" I typically put up a slide that has the following bullets that describe a few of the areas where getting data from your shop floor can help your manufacturing operations. Consider if any of these areas are possible "game changers" that would help your organization.

- Overall equipment effectiveness (OEE)
- Asset utilization
- Diagnostics
- Statistical process control
- Part production/yield
- Job/lot tracking
- Cell management
- Inspection probing
- Machine health prognostics
- Security
- Root cause analysis
- Vibration monitoring
- Preventative maintenance scheduling
- Voltage, current, power

- Energy cost predictions
- Custom reporting
- ERP interface
- Email alerts
- Anywhere, anytime access to plant floor information
- Data mining
- Genealogy

[MC]² MTConnect: Connecting Manufacturing Conference

One of the discussions that Paul Warndorf and I have on a regular basis is asking what more we can do to drive MTConnect adoption. A suggestion that I made was to have a conference for MTConnect that would be similar to the Java One conference that Sun Microsystems used to run. I thought this made sense for a number of important reasons. First, it was a great way to have a venue where we could have general sessions, both business and technical hands-on sessions, to educate individuals on MTConnect as well as have an exhibitor section so we could have the ability for MTConnect-enabled companies to show and sell their products and services. I wanted to have a creative name as well. This had to have MTConnect in the title as well as conference with the emphasis on the connect part in the word MTConnect. Finally it came to me, [MC]² MTConnect: Connecting Manufacturing Conference. The reason it is called [MC]² is that it easy to say plus it accurately represents the first letter of each of the four words. Some people call it "MC two" and some folks say "MC squared." I prefer "MC two," but as long as they show up at [MC]² I don't care what they call it. When we made the decision to have a follow-on to the first [MC]^2 in 2011, we knew we needed to get the year in the name to differentiate from other years so we call now refer to [MC]^2 as [MC]^2 2013 for example. [MC]^2 has been successful because ***tons*** of brilliant folks worked tirelessly to make it real. It has been suggested by others that [MC]^2 is a tie-back into Einstein's famous E=MC^2 equation. There is a tie in the sense that we want [MC]^2 to be a yearly event where the amount of energy coming out of the conference is truly an exponential of the speed of light. That might be a stretch, but clearly the amount of energy that has come out of [MC]^2 is extremely impressive and worth every penny of the investment that the MTConnect Institute has put into them.

What makes [MC]^2 possible is Paul's support and leadership as well as AMT's unsurpassed ability to create, manage, and run a conference. I thought we had good folks at Sun Microsystems to run conferences (and we did) but AMT's Exhibitions, Communications, and Meetings Departments all are on a whole new level. I mention all the tremendous AMT employees who make [MC]^2 in the acknowledgements section of this book.

Leonardo da Vinci, Michelangelo, Dante, and Galileo

Here's a question to ponder, "What do The Beatles, the city of Florence in Italy, and the MTConnect: Connecting Manufacturing Conference ([MC]^2)all have in common?" Since we had [MC]^2 2011 in Cincinnati, Ohio, we planned on moving [MC]^2 2013 to Florence, Italy, and having Paul McCartney and Ringo Starr as the entertainment for the opening reception. That would be nice, but it is highly unlikely. So what is the common thread? Let me explain.

There are a number of books and articles that have been written of late attempting to quantify the age-old question of "nature versus nurture" in determining someone's success. In

Malcolm Gladwell's book *Outliers*, he quantifies just how much The Beatles played together before their "instant success" appearing on *The Ed Sullivan Show* in February of 1964.[26] The Beatles played live in Hamburg, Germany, over 1,200 times from 1960 to 1964. Those nights totaled more than 10,000 hours because they were playing eight to 10 hours a night seven days a week. It would be easy to misunderstand the premise of *Outliers* if that was the only story I shared. When Gladwell was interviewed in *USA Today* in late 2008, he stated, "The biggest misconception about success is that we do it solely on our smarts, ambition, hustle, and hard work. There's an awful lot more that goes into it than we admit."[27] Gladwell emphasizes that if you want to understand why someone is successful, you also need to look beyond the nature and nurture argument, and take a look at other data points such as when and where they were born.

In Daniel Coyle's book, *The Talent Code*, Coyle discusses the question of, "why did so many incredible talents come from Florence, Italy during the renaissance?"[28] By incredibly talented, we are talking about Leonardo da Vinci, Michelangelo, Dante, and Galileo to name just a few. What was different about Florence, Italy? Guilds. What made Florence so unique were how these guilds were organized and the proven mentoring framework. Young boys were put into apprentice programs with masters that would last five to 10 years. The apprenticeship was very organized and it emphasized a hands-on approach that would build apprentices' skills from the ground up. These young artists invested thousands and thousands of hours learning their skills under the tutelage of masters.

Future [MC]²s will build upon the huge success of the inaugural conference in 2011 where we had industry thought leaders, 175 attendees, numerous speakers, hands-on labs, and 24 exhibitors. The exhibitors were demonstrating commercially available MTConnect-enabled products as well as first-time-ever demonstrations. MTConnect is a true game changer that is revolutionizing manufacturing. [MC]² will have business and technical content for a variety of individuals.

Who Should Attend [MC]²?

- Shop owners, plant managers, and anyone in manufacturing interested in improving productivity
- Industry thought leaders
- MTConnect institute participants
- Equipment Suppliers
- Students
- Professors
- Software developers
- Distributors
- ISVs
- Integrators
- Consultants
- Anyone wanting to learn more about MTConnect

As we all know, technology is a means to an end and not an end in itself. MTConnect is a set of open, royalty-free standards intended to foster greater interoperability between controls, devices, and software applications by publishing data over networks using the Internet Protocol. MTConnect is becoming the *de facto* standard for manufacturing connectivity. The most obvious application of MTConnect is to connect the shop floor to monitoring applications. It is not unusual for companies that use MTConnect to enable their shop floor to see an ROI in months and not years. It is also not unusual for those same companies that integrate the shop floor with the rest of the manufacturing enterprise to have further productivity gains. At [MC]² you will meet people from the shops and plants who have done this as well as the companies who sell MTConnect-enabled equipment and solutions.

There is a sea change happening with manufacturing and MTConnect is at the epicenter of this technology disruption. You cannot manage what you cannot measure, and MTConnect provides the plug-n-play mechanism to get real-time data off the shop or plant floor so it can be managed effectively. There are many manufacturing conferences to attend, IMTS being the granddaddy of them all in even-number years. IMTS is in the "change your schedule to be there" category of trade shows. [MC]^2 conferences are in the same category of importance as IMTS in terms of membership in the "change your schedule to be there" category. I am a little biased, but our surveys also indicated that we executed [MC]^2 2011 at a very high level with great ROI for attendees, exhibitors, and speakers.

One of the investments that we made in [MC]^2 2011 that we are making again in [MC]^2 2013 is to record all of the general, business, and technical hands-on sessions. All of these are available at MTConnect.org

In the February *AMT News* article, Mark Albert goes on to discuss the [MC]^2 2013 MTConnect: Connect Manufacturing Conference:

"Albert plans to return to [MC]^2 and thinks it's a great place to see users, suppliers, and developers all in one place. 'It really is clear that this is a practical, doable, worthwhile technology for almost any shop that's really looking for a fast payback.'"

The MTConnect Technical Advisory Group (MTCTAG) and Sun Microsystems

As described on MTConnect.org, participation on the MTCTAG (MTConnect Technical Advisory Group) is available to companies and organizations interested in taking an active role in the development of MTConnect standards and materials.

Getting in at this ground level is really an amazing way to spawn innovation at your own company as well as to reap the many evolving benefits of MTConnect.

An MTCTAG participant has both voting rights and implementer rights. Additionally, they can participate in MTCTAG working group activities. There is no fee to participate as an MTCTAG member.

To be an MTCTAG member, simply agree to the provisions of the MTConnect Intellectual Property Policy and Agreement (IP Policy). Agreeing to the IP Policy also provides participants the rights to implement MTConnect in product offerings and services. You can download the IP Policy from MTConnect.org.

Sun Microsystems realized the benefits of joining MTCTAG, a decision that many in the IT and software development industry should emulate. The reason Sun benefited is because it now had a vote and clear voice in the MTConnect Institute on decisions being made. Sun had an interest in the MTConnect-enabled data coming out of these machine tools for doing analytics, and Sun had embedded Java processors that could act as MTConnect-enabled sensors.

SANTA CLARA, Calif.—(Business Wire) Sun Microsystems, Inc. (Nasdaq:JAVA) announced today that it will join the MTConnect Technical Advisory Group (MTCTAG) to further define the open communication protocol standard it helped create for the manufacturing technology industry a year ago.

MTConnect is an open manufacturing technology standard that uses proven, royalty free Internet communications technologies as its basis to allow manufacturing technology vendors and customers to safely and easily communicate.

"Sun Microsystems has a very long history of working with the industry and academia to create and promote open

technology standards that drive genuine innovation," said Dave Edstrom, Chief Technologist of the Americas Software Practice for Sun Microsystems. "Open source and open standards are the keys to unlocking manufacturing innovation and efficiency around the world, particularly in growing emerging markets. I am thrilled Sun has been able to play a pivotal role in the development of such an important initiative as MTConnect."

The Challenge in Today's Manufacturing Facilities and Machine Shops

A typical manufacturing facility includes hundreds, if not thousands, of machines and autonomous systems that must operate together to produce high-quality products in a timely and cost-effective manner. While each of these machines and systems accumulates information on its operation, this data cannot usually be shared, which makes it difficult to track machine efficiency, process flow, energy usage, toolpath validation, and other metrics. As a result, manufacturers are challenged to coordinate and optimize machines and systems to ensure that these individual components and the factory as a whole are operating at acceptable levels.

Interoperability from Design Studio to Shop Floor

MTConnect is an essential first step to connect these production islands and will open up new markets and opportunities for the manufacturing technology industry. Bringing unprecedented interoperability from design studio to shop floor, MTConnect helps enable third-party solution providers to develop software and hardware that make the entire manufacturing enterprise much more productive.

With MTConnect, the manufacturing technology industry can mirror the success of the information technology industry, where common, open industry standards are used to design hardware and software technology to enable different manufacturers' products to work with each other. Just as large compute farms are used to accurately model microprocessors today, MTConnect should help enable the vision of "art to part, first-time correct" by taking advantage of large compute clusters.

Sun's Leadership

As a leader in creating open standards for the IT industry, Sun is in a strong position to help the manufacturing industry create a common, open standard. The Solaris™ Operating System, Java™ technology, the Sun Java Real-Time System, Sun™ SPOT, Sun™ xVM software and MySQL™ software are among the innovative technologies that will help enable MTConnect to deliver complete and open interoperability on the manufacturing floor, seamlessly connecting to the enterprise as well as to technology manufacturing partners in ways that were previously impossible.

Sun's long history of innovation in CAD/CAM, HPC, grid computing, simulation, real-time and modeling technology provides the ideal platform for MTConnect. Indeed, manufacturing technology companies could have immediate access to Sun computing resources via the Network.com Software Catalogue platform, allowing them to easily build, test, and deploy MTConnect enabled applications on-demand over the Internet.

MTConnect History

Although developed through an open collaborative effort, the MTConnect initiative was initially led by Dr. Dave Patterson, Professor in Computer Science of the University of California at Berkeley, and Sun's Dave Edstrom.

Edstrom was inspired to approach Dr. Patterson after attending the International Manufacturing Technology Show (IMTS) in September 2006. "I was absolutely convinced that creating a manufacturing technology standard using proven, open and royalty-free Internet technologies was an imperative effort in which Sun must invest," he said. "The expected impact of MTConnect on the manufacturing sector is analogous to the effect that the browser had on the development of the Internet: MTConnect will revolutionize the manufacturing technology industry by providing a common, open platform which, in turn, will revolutionize manufacturing."

Dr. Patterson commented, "It is great news for the manufacturing technology industry that MTConnect is becoming real, and that Sun Microsystems will be officially joining the MTConnect Advisory Group."

"Sun recognized the potential of utilizing the power of information technology to move manufacturing to levels of productivity never seen before," added John Byrd, President of the Association for Manufacturing Technology. "When the history of MTConnect is written, Sun Microsystems will be recognized as having played a critical role in the development of the initial concept. Dave Edstrom's vision and foresight enabled thought leaders of our industry to step out of their comfort zone and tackle the most significant issue the manufacturing technology industry will face in the 21st Century."

MTConnect will be demonstrated at next week's International Manufacturing Technology Show (IMTS 2008).

About Sun Microsystems

Sun Microsystems develops the technologies that power the global marketplace. Guided by a singular vision—"The Network Is The Computer"—Sun drives network participation through *shared innovation, community development, and open source leadership. Sun can be found in more than 100 countries and on the Web at http://sun.com.*

Sun, Sun Microsystems, the Sun logo, Java, Solaris, MySQL, Network.com and The Network Is The Computer are trademarks or registered trademarks of Sun Microsystems, Inc. or its subsidiaries in the United States and other countries.

Chapter 8: MTConnect Basics

Manufacturing Before and After MTConnect

You have read about the need for a shift in thinking in manufacturing and have been told some great examples from the computer science industry. We've covered some possible tools at your disposal, such as cloud computing and monitoring systems. Now it is time to roll up our sleeves and really get into the detail of MTConnect since it is the key component needed to ensure you take part in this great shift in manufacturing, that you embrace an open system, and that you monitor and improve.

You've also trudged through a lot of words up to now. So, before the explanations get really detailed, let's pause to consider MTConnect at the highest, simplest level through a few explanatory images.

Turn the page to see a "before MTConnect" picture (see Figure 6).

Figure 6. *The manufacturing world prior to MTConnect.*

Notice in Figure 6 that each machine tool speaks a
different language. In Figure 7, you will notice that the number
of connections is the classic *n*-squared problem of connectivity.
This was a nightmare for software application developers.
Prior to MTConnect, the onus was software developers to have
to write an adapter for each and every piece of manufacturing
equipment on the shop floor that the customer was trying to
collect data from. MTConnect takes the burden from the
application developer and moves it where it should be—closer
to the device itself.

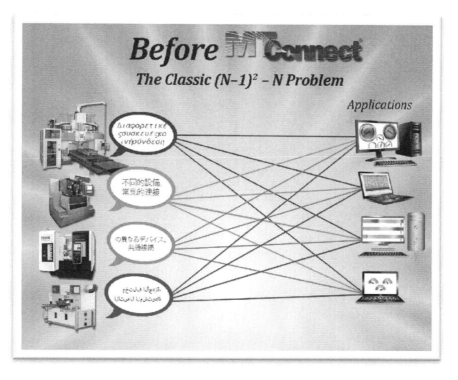

Figure 7. *The classic (N-1)² – N problem.*

Figure 8 shows (at a very high level) how MTConnect addresses this issue. From a developer standpoint, the problem of converting the proprietary formats has been moved from the adapter layer closer to the actual piece of manufacturing equipment. The advantage of this to the application developer is that now with MTConnect each client application only needs to concern itself with speaking MTConnect.

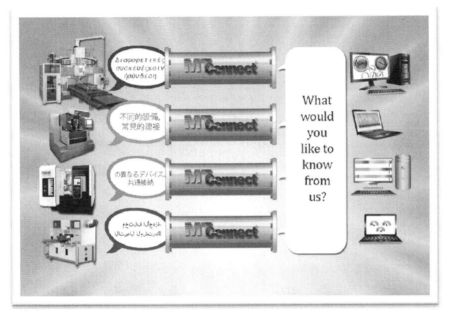

Figure 8. *MTConnect is the Bluetooth for connecting manufacturing equipment to applications.*

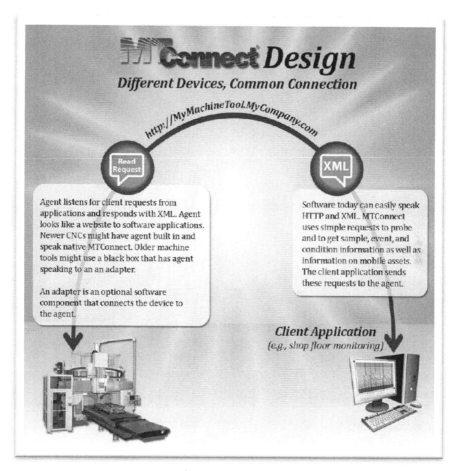

Figure 9. *The client-agent-adapter manufacturing equipment relationship.*

MTConnect: An Overview

What is MTConnect?

MTConnect is an open and royalty-free standard for manufacturing that is connecting manufacturing equipment with applications by using proven Internet protocols. As I state earlier, please think of MTConnect as the Bluetooth for manufacturing. With Bluetooth, both devices must speak Bluetooth for anything useful to happen. Just as simply having an OBD-II port on your car does not provide you with any more data unless you have an OBD-II scanner, the same "pairing" principle applies to MTConnect and software applications. You can have an MTConnect-enabled machine tool or piece of manufacturing equipment, but without the software to read and analyze the data you do not have both sides of the equation. The OBD-II scanner is really the application or the tool that you use to help you understand what is happening with your engine. In manufacturing, it is software applications, such as shop floor monitoring programs, that are the applications that speak to an MTConnect-enabled piece of manufacturing equipment on the shop floor.

What Isn't MTConnect?

MTConnect is not an application. Let me say that again, MTConnect is not an application. MTConnect is not a product. The MTConnect Institute does not sell MTConnect. MTConnect is a standard based on open and royalty-free protocols. This is a common point of confusion with non-software developers. Paul Warndorf likes to tell the story of the individual at IMTS 2010 who pulled out their credit card and wanted to buy MTConnect. It was analogous to a shopper in Best Buy pulling out their credit card and wanting to buy Bluetooth. It is natural to understand where the confusion comes in because MTConnect in and of itself is simply the plug-n-play for making it easy to get data from manufacturing equipment. However, it is what you ***do*** with that data that turns the MTConnect data into actionable intelligence.

The MTConnect Standard

The MTConnect standard is broken down into four parts. What follows are the four standard sections of MTConnect and its major subsections. Later, we will explore what the software developer needs to know in order get data from an MTConnect-enabled device. Before the developer is able to develop anything more than a very simple application, it will be necessary read and understand Parts 1, 2, and 3 of the standard. Part 4 is for assets and this becomes important for developers who are using those typically "mobile" assets of the manufacturing equipment.

MTConnect Standard Part 1

- Overview and Protocol
- MTConnect Document Structure
- Versioning
- HTTP and XML—Brief Reminder
- Architecture Overview
- Request Structure
- Agent Initialization
- Application Communication
- Agent Data and Agent Asset Storage
- Reply XML Document Structure
- Devices
- Streams
- Assets
- Error
- Protocol (Commands to Agent) Overview
- Probe
- Sample
- Current
- Asset

- MTConnect Agent and Adapters

MTConnect Standard Part 2

- Components
- Data Items

MTConnect Standard Part 3

- Streams
- Events
- Samples
- Conditions

MTConnect Standard Part 4

- Assets

Licensing and Selling MTConnect

Please go to MTConnect.org for complete information. Neither this book nor this section is intended or designed to be a substitute for reading all of the necessary and most current licensing information on MTConnect.

Below is a paragraph from the beginning of many MTConnect documents that describes the *essence* of adopting or implementing MTConnect: "If you intend to adopt or implement an MTConnect® Specification or Material in a product, whether hardware, software or firmware which complies with an MTConnect® Specification, you SHALL agree to the MTConnect® Specification Implementer License Agreement ("Implementer License") or to the MTConnect® Intellectual Property Policy and Agreement ("IP Policy"). The Implementer License and IP Policy each sets forth the license terms and other terms of use for MTConnect® Implementers to adopt or implement the MTConnect® Specifications, including certain license rights covering necessary patent claims for that purpose. These materials can be found at www.MTConnect.org, or by contacting Paul Warndorf at pwarndorf@mtconnect.hyperoffice.com."

It is strongly encouraged to read and understand the MTConnect Intellectual Property Policy and Agreement, MTConnect Specification Implementers License Agreement, the source code and binary FAQ at MTConnect.org, as well as read the licensing text file at github.com/MTConnect. The first three documents above are located under the "Institute" drop down on the first page and then select the "Join Us" page.

There is sometimes confusion on MTConnect and pricing. The MTConnect Institute places its source code and binaries at github.com and there is no fee to download. It is important to read the licensing text file at github.com/MTConnect, which is called LICENSE.TXT. When you open this file, you will see the MTConnect Specification Implementer License Agreement for MTConnect. A very important point is that what our MTCTAG members or implementers decide to do with MTConnect, from a pricing standpoint, is totally up to them. They can give it away or charge whatever they would like for it. It is their business decision.

Specifically, here is just one section from the Intellectual Property Policy and Agreement that deals with this topic:

"Confirm that Implementers have no obligation to make their own products based on MTConnect "open" and/or available for free—MTConnect Specifications set minimum requirements for interoperability, and developers are free to innovate and add proprietary value to MTConnect-compliant products."

Again, go to MTConnect.org as well as github.com/MTConnect and download and read all of the necessary forms and documents.

MTConnect Institute's Mission

Below is directly from MTConnect.org:

"The MTConnect Institute is a not-for-profit 501(c)(6) organization established to further the development of the MTConnect standard and publish related materials. The organization includes a Board of Directors, a Technical Advisory Group that's also called MTCTAG, a Technical Steering Committee, as well as various working groups to further the standard in specific technology areas."

As is also defined on MTConnect.org, "MTConnect Institute's mission is to enable the manufacturing  industry to reach its fullest potential by developing standards and guidelines that ensure the longtime growth of the industry. This is accomplished by the creation of standards to foster greater interoperability between devices and manufacturing intelligence software applications."

Funding the Future of MTConnect

MTConnect is funded by ALL of its members. There is a misconception that AMT is the only entity that funds MTConnect and that AMT has an unlimited bank account. While it would be nice if the MTConnect Institute had a few billion dollars of cash on hand, as president and chairman of the board for the MTConnect Institute, I can tell you that we don't. AMT has been very generous in its leadership and support of MTConnect, but if we want to continue to grow MTConnect, it will take funding and expertise from all of its members, industry, the government, and those who are benefiting from MTConnect.

It is important to point out the differences between how the computer industry funds standard efforts and how manufacturing funds standard efforts. When Sun started Java, Sun did everything from creating Java, marketing it, educating people, running conferences, creating the Java Community Process (JCP), and countless other items that were needed to make Java successful. It was very exciting times during those early days. What happened next is that Sun recruited other companies to join the Java revolution. These companies joined initially because of Java's promise of "Write Once, Run Anywhere." This was a huge change in traditional software development. What happened after that was interesting to watch, Sun no longer had to recruit companies, companies came to Sun. These companies did two things, they invested their company's time and money in developing Java products, but more importantly these companies sent their best software developers to work on Java. These companies do not expect Sun to pay for their own software developers to work on Java. The reason for this is that the companies know that by providing software developers that Java can grow and that growth will help everyone including their own company's efforts.

Java and MTConnect share an important trait in that they are both simply a means to an end. Java by itself is useless. MTConnect by itself is useless. However, when a software developer uses Java to create applications and run those applications on any type of device or computer, that is a game changer. The same applies to MTConnect when it is put on the shop floor and then an application is MTConnect enabled. At that point MTConnect is the enabling technology that provides a lens on what is happening on the shop floor and that lens can be focused to improve productivity and that information can be integrated, analyzed and used in the decision making process.

Where there is a huge difference between the funding for Java and MTConnect is the number of software developers who are made available. With Java, there was no shortage of talented software developers that companies would provide to help build Java. At the MTConnect Institute, we don't have that luxury and need to pay for software developers because most in manufacturing want to keep their talented software developers working at their own companies. As we go forward, we need to indoctrinate that Java culture into MTConnect so that companies will realize that it is to their benefit to send their talented software developers to work on new versions of MTConnect. This is critical for MTConnect to keep growing.

Any organization that is building a standard needs to have a recurring funding stream. One of the purposes of the [MC]^2 conferences is to provide some of the needed funding for the MTConnect Institute that is used to build the standard and market MTConnect. Paul Warndorf has done an outstanding job acquiring funding sources for MTConnect. As MTConnect continues to grow, the financial goal is for multiple recurring revenue streams. At the first [MC]^2 in 2011, we were able to make money from this conference, and every dime went back into the standard. The same will apply with [MC]^2 2013. We are very thankful for all of the companies that have invested in MTConnect in a variety of ways. It is exciting to witness the number of organizations that are helping MTConnect continue to grow and my hope is that we will see a big increase in the software developers that companies will make available to help build the standard.

MTConnect Forum

I strongly encourage everyone who has questions on MTConnect to go to MTConnectForum.com; this is where all the MTConnect experts hang out. We want the MTConnect Forum to turn into the equivalent of the Corvette Forum. When you want to discuss, learn, question, or pontificate on Corvettes you go to Corvette Forum, we want the MTConnect Forum to be thought of in that same vein.

Product Locator

The product locator at MTConnect.org is a great place to find out which companies have MTConnect-enabled products and services. Figure 10 shows how the product locator makes it easy to find products. Thanks to Paul Warndorf for driving this important aspect of MTConnect to reality.

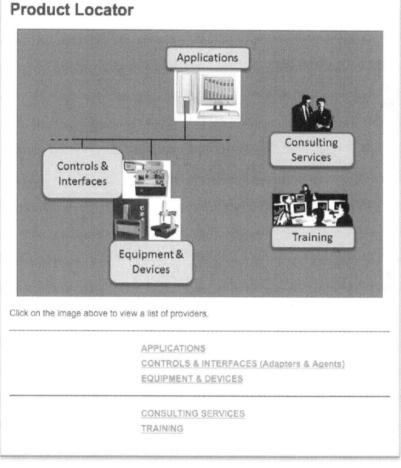

Figure 10. *The product locator as seen on MTConnect.org.*

Chapter 9: What Software Developers Need to Know About MTConnect

For those who just want a white paper that was written for software developers, these next few chapters are for you. The primary intended audience for these chapters is really focused on the developers who are not in the manufacturing arena, but who are interested in creating MTConnect client applications. The reason for this focus is that these chapters were written with the specific goal of expanding the number of software developers for MTConnect and hopefully the number of interesting applications that are created for MTConnect-enabled manufacturing equipment and devices.

If you are a software developer in the manufacturing arena, this will be a very helpful primer to learn about MTConnect, but you might be better served to simply read the MTConnect specification—Parts 1, 2, 3, and 4. If you are not a software developer and not in manufacturing, the first part would give you a high-level architecture overview, but there are other documents at MTConnect.org you would find more appropriate. If your interests are more business related, you may better benefit from the white papers and many videos that we have at MTConnect.org.

This section should be viewed as a primer and a companion document to the actual MTConnect Specification. Please note this section will be receiving additional updates and clarifications over time. As of this writing, the current MTConnect specification is version 1.2.

Five years ago Dr. Armando Fox wrote on this same topic, but I wanted to update the ideas introduced in his white paper with both the information I gleaned from the MTConnect Challenge (which I explain in a moment) and conversations I had with my oldest John, who is a gifted software developer at Facebook and was a developer at Microsoft working on Windows 8 security, but knows little about manufacturing. We need to get the John Edstrom's of the world developing MTConnect applications. Currently 99.9999 percent of software developers are not in the manufacturing arena, and we need to get them interested and educated. Why? Manufacturing is absolutely ripe for creative integration through new applications. MTConnect is becoming a huge enabler for manufacturing on the shop floor. Note that at MTConnect.org, there is a white paper I wrote called, "Getting Started With MTConnect: Writing Client Applications" which is strictly for software developers and in particular the huge world of software developers who are not in manufacturing but want to understand how MTConnect works and how to write client applications for MTConnect.

One of the most important events ever in the history of MTConnect is the MTConnect Challenge, which is comprised of two main goals (per the National Center for Defense Manufacturing and Machining [NCDMM] website):

1. "To engage and stimulate a broader base of software and system architects to develop advanced enterprise, facility, and machine control applications based on, and extensions to, the MTConnect standard to enable a more efficient and competitive domestic manufacturing infrastructure for the defense enterprise; and"

2. "To create valuable tools and applications that can be easily adopted by manufacturing enterprises, especially the lower-tier producers, to enhance their manufacturing capabilities and support Department of Defense (DoD) supply chain management goals."

This challenge will be discussed in detail at [MC]² 2013. In my opinion the main obstacle for the MTConnect Challenge to be successful is to make sure that the broadest group of experienced software developers can quickly understand the world of manufacturing so they can enter the challenge. I wrote this section for the experienced software developer who knows nothing about manufacturing. Again, we need to broaden the number of software developers who are working in manufacturing and with MTConnect.

What is the definition of an experienced software developer? An individual who has multiple years of hands-on experience with software programming languages such as Java, C, C++, C#, or other high-level programming languages, as well as extensive experience with web services, SAX, DOM, REST, XML, and http. This description could also be described as the type of software background that most companies would expect when hiring a software developer.

What if the reader does not have expertise in the languages and protocols stated above? The Internet is overflowing with sites where the reader can learn more about these languages and protocols. The reader can also go to MTConnectForum.com for questions regarding MTConnect's client development. Without a software developer's background, Chapters 10 and 11 will have limited value to the reader unless the goal is simply a high-level overview.

What this book and this section does not assume is that the reader has a deep of understanding of manufacturing equipment or what happens on the shop floor. Why? Simply put, we want to expand the pool of MTConnect-enabled applications outside of manufacturing software companies. Shop floor monitoring is the obvious first step, but it is exactly that—a first step. The true value of MTConnect comes about when the data coming off the shop floor is not used for just shop floor monitoring, but also when it is integrated into the total manufacturing enterprise. The shop floor monitoring software companies have figured out how to use MTConnect by reading the standard. Some have attended classes given by

Will Sobel, the chief architect for MTConnect and president of System Insights. Some have learned on their own by going to the MTConnect section of gitub that is located at https://github.com/mtconnect.

While it is obvious that it would be very helpful to have deep manufacturing domain knowledge, it is not critical for the reader to have deep expertise of manufacturing. Deep expertise of manufacturing is needed if the reader intends to write an MTConnect agent or adapter. This is not to diminish the value of this domain knowledge, but you don't have to have been a machinist in order to write an application to get data off a machine tool. In the same way that a software developer does not need to be a neurosurgeon to write a medical application, the same is true of writing MTConnect client applications. However, the software developer does need to have baseline knowledge of the nature of the business domain and this chapter will provide high-level domain overview and pointers to additional documents and resources. This next section will discuss agents and adapters from a high level; it is not a guide to writing MTConnect agents or adapters.

Three Key Pillars of MTConnect Architecture

From a software developer's perspective and at an 80,000-foot view, MTConnect has three key pillars:

1. Adapter
2. Agent
3. Application

Applications speak to an agent. The agent speaks to adapters (adapters are optional). Adapters or agents speak to manufacturing equipment.

Adapter

The adapter is the optional piece of software that can be thought of as the bridge between the manufacturing equipment and the agent. On one side, the adapter is speaking whatever protocol, as well as providing whatever physical mechanism, that is needed to speak to a piece of manufacturing equipment (could be a machine tool, bar feeder, Coordinate Measuring Machine [CMM], etc.), normalizing that data, putting it into a modified version of the Simple Hierarchical Data Representation (SHDR) format, and sending it to the agent. The SHDR protocol is a simple flat, fast, and low-latency, human-readable protocol delimited by pipes (|) that is in ISO 8601 date-time format with optional decimal places. The adapter is optional because for those pieces of manufacturing equipment where MTConnect is native, there is no need for an adapter.

Below are some key points to remember about MTConnect adapters. MTConnect adapters:

- Do not appear in the MTConnect standard
- Are optional (for non-native MTConnect devices)
- Speak to devices on one side of the equation
- Constantly stream output to agent(s)
- Typically do not speak to applications directly as this would involve bypassing the agent which makes little logical sense
- Can send data to multiple agents or just one agent—it is a design and implementation choice

The big picture is that adapters speak to an agent(s) on one side of the equation and manufacturing equipment on the other.

The reference adapter is the adapter that the MTConnect Institute provides at the MTConnect location on github.com. What sometimes is confusing is that the MTConnect Institute provides a reference adapter and a reference agent to make it easy for developers to create these two pieces of software.

Keep in mind that "reference" means it is either a binary or the source code that you can use to develop your agent or adapter. You can *refer* to it as you develop your own adapters or agents. This is a standard type of model used in software development. What confuses those outside of software is whether or not the MTConnect Institute mandates the reference agent or adapter—the answer to that is no. A software developer could simply read the MTConnect standard and write their own agents and adapters without ever viewing the reference software. It has been proven that by providing the reference adapters and agents we have decreased the development time for those who are writing MTConnect agents and adapters.

The difficulty in writing an adapter varies from very easy and quick to very difficult and time consuming. The reason for the range is:

- How much documentation do you have for the device you are trying to connect?
- What is the physical medium that is needed to get information?
- Is there a similar adapter that has been written?
- How much information are you trying to get out?
- Are the costs to get the documentation prohibitive?

Also consider the following examples of reference adapter and agent responsibilities.

1. The term "reference" agent is used loosely in this context because there is no standard for an adapter. This was done by design. While this is true, it is also true that many agent developers have used the SHDR protocol as the mechanism for the adapter to send data to the agent. Again, we give flexibility to the developers.

2. Adapters can provide a socket connection to which a process can connect and receive updates.

3. Adapters only send data when it changes (this is very important) and only sends data after handshake with agent. In other words, the adapter will not just send out data with no known agent.

4. Adapters should make sure all data conforms to a controlled vocabulary, fixed set of values, and only communicate those values. Examples are ControllerMode and Execution.

5. Agents can support multiple connections for testing.

6. Agents send all initial values to new clients when they connect.

7. Adapters format the data according to the SHDR specification.

8. There is a heartbeat between the reference adapter and agent. For example:

   - Agent sends a **ping** to the adapter.

   - Adapter responds with a **"pong."**

     - If the agent does not receive a pong, then first assumption is this is a legacy adapter, if no response after 20 seconds then agent considers adapter to be dead.

   - There is a heartbeat between both adapter and agent every 10 seconds, but that can be changed.

   - IF one does not respond to the other's heartbeat for two times the interval, then that [agent/adapter] is considered dead.

9. Adapters perform the connection(s) to the manufacturing equipment interfaces and gather data.

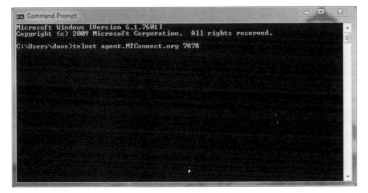

Figure 11. *Talking directly to an adapter.*

Figure 11 above shows the simplicity of talking to the adapter by using the standard telnet command. The user can simply telnet to the port defined for your adapter and see output that is going to the agent. This is very helpful for troubleshooting when you are developing your adapters and agents or you simply want to verify the adapter is putting out data.

Figure 12. *The output of the adapter. Above is SHDR output.*

Noticed that the reference adapter output is very simple and is delimited by |. The agent is reading the adapter output, puts in a buffer that can then be read from an MTConnect-enabled application or from any application that can speak HTTP and read XML—such as a simple browser.

Below are a few examples of what comes out of the adapter. I wanted to show the reader what to expect when they telnet to the adapter, but since that is a little hard to read in the graphic, I also include below for clarity.

2012-08-20T01:34:21.650493|Xact|-1.7883759737|Yact|-
   0.3661781847|Xcom|-1.7899452213|Ycom|-0.3595617390

2012-08-20T01:34:21.666492|Xact|-1.7894827127|Yact|-
   0.3615075648|Xcom|-1.7908221776|Ycom|-
   0.3556611774|path_feedrate|0.3061054894

2012-08-20T01:34:21.682492|Xact|-1.7905533314|Yact|-
0.3568308055|Xcom|-1.7916012147|Ycom|-
0.3517520805|path_feedrate|0.2972257736

The screen will be racing by with this type of information coming above from the adapter. The sampling rate is determined by the adapter.

NOTE: This connection to the machine tool interface and the gathering of data is where all of the hard and time-consuming work is done. Remember, the adapter is **not** part of the standard and this just provides background on the reference adapter.

Agent

The agent can be thought of as very efficient web server that bridges between adapter(s) and application(s). As a developer of client applications, expertise in what the agent is doing and understanding the standard is critical.

The agent "represents" one or more MTConnect-compliant machines. It makes machine data available in uniform MTConnect representations, responds to MTConnect commands, and allows clients to specify/select which data is of interest. The agent can "listen" to multiple adapters. Figure 13 is a picture of what the agent is doing.

Figure 13. *The agent "bucket" buffer model.*

Think of the agent as having two buckets or buffers that the controller deposits data into

- SamplesEventsConditions Buffer default is 131,072 which is also known as 2^{17}. NOTE: This must be a factor of two for speed purposes.
- Assets Buffer default is 1,024.
- Both buffers can be changed in size.

Both of these can be changed to different sizes based on need. Each application "reaches into the bucket" at the rate it wants. As the bucket fills up, older measurements "leak out" the bottom depending on whether or not any applications have read them and the capacity of bucket, which depends on agent implementation.

The ability to keep or persist the data can be done either at the application level or by creating a custom agent—whichever is the developer's design choice

Application

The application or client is the software that speaks directly to the agent, requesting information and keeping track of the sequence numbers so it can continue to request and process XML information coming from the agent. The most obvious application when connecting to a piece of manufacturing equipment is shop floor monitoring software. A shop floor monitoring program typically requests information from the agent(s), processes that information, and then displays graphs or charts on what the piece of manufacturing equipment is doing.

What is interesting for software developers is all the ways MTConnect data can be analyzed in the countless other non-shop floor applications.

Legacy Through New: Connecting Different Types of Devices with MTConnect

As a developer of an MTConnect client application or someone who simply wants to understand how we differentiate the types of manufacturing equipment on the shop floor, you will need to understand the high-level differences of the three types of device connections.

MTConnect Native Device

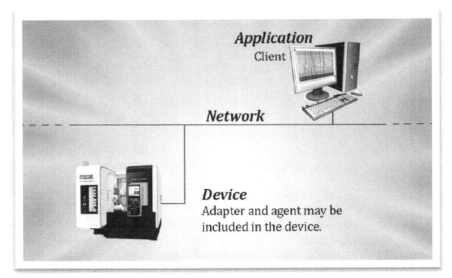

Figure 14. *MTConnect Native Device.*

Above is a diagram of a piece of manufacturing equipment (remember, not just machine tools) with MTConnect native on the device. What this simply means is that this device comes with an MTConnect agent already included in the device and an MTConnect-enabled application could immediately speak to this device with no additional software or hardware that is needed. Native MTConnect devices would be newer devices as MTConnect was first released to the outside world at the end of 2008.

MTConnect Translation-Dependent Device

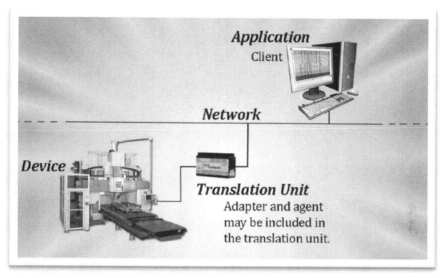

Figure 15. *MTConnect Translation-Dependent Device.*

Figure 15 presents a diagram of a MTConnect Translation-Dependent Device. What this means is that there is a device, which could be hardware and/or software, that acts a translator between whatever proprietary hardware and/or software interface that the manufacturing equipment speaks and MTConnect applications.

An example of this might be a small black box that runs Linux and has both an adapter and an agent running. The black box might also have a number of ports on it to speak to a wide variety of protocols as well as have one or more Ethernet ports on it. The adapter speaks to the manufacturing equipment using the physical port and protocol that the manufacturing equipment understands and then that adapter sends information to the agent using the SHDR protocol. The agent then takes that information and makes it available in a MTConnect-compliant format. A specific example of this might be a black box that has a FANUC FOCAS adapter that is speaking to a FANUC CNC controller as well as the MTConnect

151

agent on the same box that is accepting SHDR from the adapter and then making it available to MTConnect-enabled applications.

The key part of a MTConnect Translation-Dependent Device is that the adapter is typically speaking to an Application Programming Interface (API) to send queries to that device, translating that information into SHDR, and then sending it to the MTConnect agent. There are many examples of this where the CNC controller speaks a specific protocol and you most likely need to license a Software Development Kit (SDK) or software library to be able to speak to the CNC controller in the language that it knows. There are a variety of adapters at gitub.com/MTConnect

Please note that the adapter is not part of the MTConnect standard and in the example above I am referring to the reference adapter.

MTConnect Connection-Dependent Device

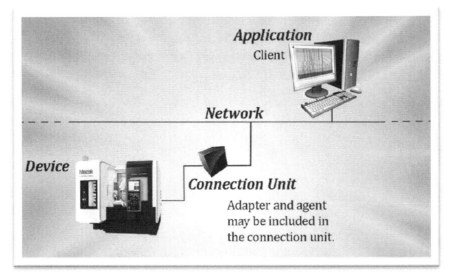

Figure 16. *MTConnect Connection-Dependent Device.*

Figure 16 is a diagram of a piece of manufacturing that is known as a MTConnect Connection-Dependent Device. What this means is that there is a device that could be hardware and/or software that acts a translator between whatever proprietary hardware and/or software interface that the manufacturing equipment speaks and MTConnect applications. Sometimes there is confusion between a Translation Unit and a Connection Unit. Here is the key difference: the Translation Unit Device is speaking to a device that has an API whereas a Connection Unit has no API. This typically means a Connection Unit is talking to an older piece of manufacturing equipment and pulling off very low-level signals, such as doing an A/D conversion, that are then transformed and sent to the agent. The simplest example of this might be an old lathe. The only piece of data that can be easily derived is whether the lathe is off, on, or in the process of cutting. A connection unit would have the appropriate ports to determine whether it was off, on, or in the process of cutting and the adapter would pass the information along to the agent. The agent then would respond to client requests where only those three data items could be requested. While it might be argued that only knowing those three are not that helpful, the truth is that it is much better than a stack light, and even with this low-level example of MTConnect enabling a simple device there are advantages above and beyond a stack light replacement. For example, with the electrical information, the costs of running that lathe could easily be calculated. Now the manufacturer knows the electrical cost of that device, what percent of the time the device is running and not running. There are MTConnect Connection Unit black boxes that are literally plug-n-play for these type of older pieces of manufacturing equipment.

How do you know what agents are available for which pieces of manufacturing equipment? Hopefully, the IT department is using DNS, Active Directory, or some similar dynamic discovery mechanism. In order to make it easy to write an MTConnect client, the MTConnect Institute has paid for a simulator at MTConnect.Agent.org. Some vendors also supply MTConnect simulators that can be used for testing as well. This document will use MTConnect.Agent.org to show the MTConnect commands.

Programmatic Conceptual Terms

The terms below are key conceptual terms that software developers will need to know and understand when developing an application that will speak to the MTConnect agent.

- **Header.** Protocol-related information.

- **Components**. The building blocks of the device.

- **Data Items.** The description of the data available from the device.

- **Streams.** A set of samples or events for components and devices.

- **Samples.** A point-in-time measurement of a data item that is continuously changing.

- **Events.** Unexpected or discrete occurrence in a component. This includes state changes and conditions.

- **Conditions Are Normal, Warning, or Fault.** Warning is trending toward a fault and fault means the device has stopped and needs intervention to get it working.

MTConnect's Powerful Data Dictionary

A very powerful component of the MTConnect standard (tons of hard work went into creating this) is the XML schema or the data dictionary. The file http://www.mtconnect.org/schemas/MTConnectDevices_1.2.xsd is over 600 lines long. It is this data dictionary that makes the job of the client application developer much easier. Applications that do not provide a schema place the burden on determining what each value means, as well as the allowable values, back onto the shoulders of the application developer. Figure 17 drives home this point.

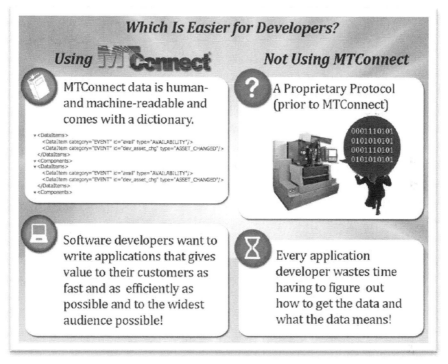

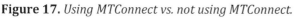

Figure 17. *Using MTConnect vs. not using MTConnect.*

In Figure 17, notice that AssetCountAttrType is "The number of assets," it is an integer that has a minimum value of 0 and a maximum value of 4,294,967,295. I doubt 4,294,967,295 will be a limit for assets anytime in my lifetime.

It is impossible to over emphasize the importance and the time that went into creating MTConnect's powerful name space or data dictionary. It takes years and thousands of man-hours to do it properly. There are standards out there that do not supply a data dictionary and place the entire burden of knowing what bits are coming to the application on the software developer writing client applications

You may wonder, "How does one making suggestions for additions to the MTConnect standard?" There is a very good white paper at MTConnect.org titled, "Recommending the Addition of Devices, Components, and Data Items to the MTConnect Standard" that addresses this question.

The Simplest MTConnect Clients—Your Browser and a Spreadsheet

The first step in understanding how to write an MTConnect client application is to understand how to speak to the agent.

To do so, you can literally type the name of your machine tool into your browser. To see how this might work, there is a machine tool simulator running at agent.MTConnect.org. Go to http://agent.MTConnect.org/probe to try it out.

You can literally type the name of your machine tool into Excel and start reading and charting MTConnect data. How? Excel speaks HTTP and XML like all applications that were not written in a cave.

MTConnect reads manufacturing equipment data (from a machine tool for example, but it could be any type of device on the shop floor) and converts it to XML.

Below are the very easy steps to get MTConnect data into Excel:

- Go into the Data selection on the upper tab.
- Select From Web.
- New Web Query will come up.
- In the browser bar that pops up, put in your MTConnect http url, for example:
    - http://agent.mtconnect.org/sample?count=1000
- Hit Import.

- You will then hit Import again after the data is loaded into the window.

- Select Yes to add to the question, "Do You Want To Continue To Add This Schema To Your Notebook?"

- When the popup window comes up for Import Data, select Existing Worksheet which is the bottom selection when you are promoted on where to put your data.

- At this point Excel will put in the proper headers and values in the correct locations.

Of course, you will likely want to use a more specific Sample Request in step #4, but I kept it simple to just to make the point how easy it is for applications to get data from an MTConnect enabled device. This is the beautiful aspect of MTConnect: it is brain-dead easy to talk to an MTConnect agent. It is so easy that even an Excel spreadsheet can be a simple MTConnect client. While you would not use this in production, the point is that MTConnect makes it very, very easy to get the data.

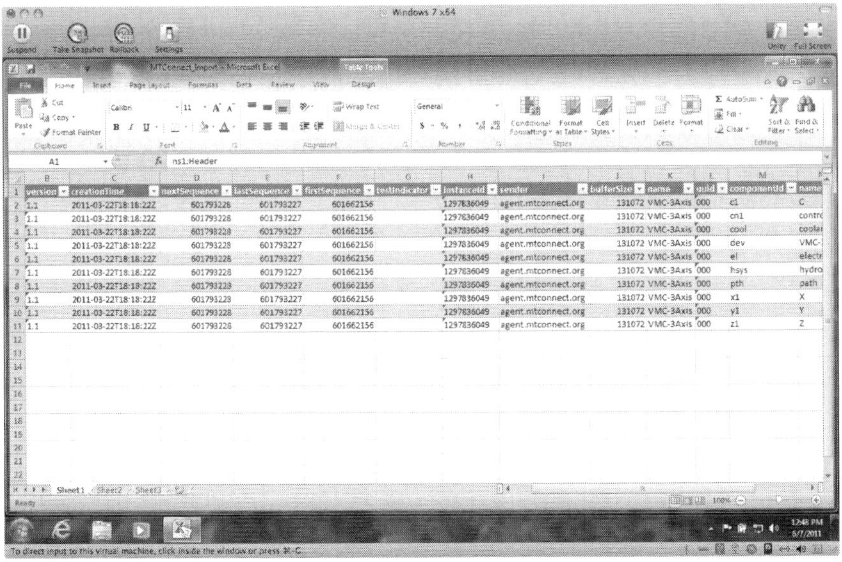

Figure 18. *An Excel spreadsheet as an MTConnect client.*

If you'd like to view a four-minute screencast on exactly how to do this, go to **http://tinyurl.com/EasyMTConnect.** Notice that I did absolutely nothing in terms of laying out the titles of the columns, where the columns and rows should go, or where the data should appear. Since this is XML, Excel (just like a lot of software that reads XML data) knows how to deal with the data and display it properly.

Chapter 10: MTConnect Under the Hood

Fault Tolerance and Persistence of Data

MTConnect was designed to be simple and scalable. MTConnect uses a RESTful protocol—meaning it is stateless on the server side much like a Network File System (NFS). Sun Microsystems created NFS to have a universal way to share data on a network. Prior to NFS, systems had to use tools such as File Transfer Protocol (FTP) where you were required to copy each and every file from one system to the system you wanted to use the file at. The problem with ftping files is that you had one file at the source system and another copy at the destination system. As soon as either changed, you were out of sync. The other options were proprietary sharing of software systems. NFS is a stateless protocol. This means that every time an NFS client speaks to an NFS server, the two systems act is if it were the first time. While this might sound like a disadvantage, in the real world this is a huge advantage because you remove the complexity of having to store all the current state of a transaction either on the server or the client.

Stateless protocol is the foundation of REST or REpresentational State Transfer. REST is the world's worst acronym in my opinion because neither the acronym nor the words that it stands for really explains the beauty of REST. REST keeps conversations simple. Applications that have a REST-like interface are referred to as RESTful. Simple always wins when writing scalable software and this is why REST is so widely adopted on the web today.

There is NO fault tolerance or automated recovery for MTConnect. It is up to the agent or the application to keep track of and persist any data. The reference agent does not

159

persist data. A circular buffer is defined where the adapter is writing data.

When developing clients, you should ask how the adapters (which are optional) and the agents are restarted in case of failure. Are they defined as services that are automatically restarted? While the adapters and agents are outside the scope of this overview, it is still important to understand what happens with adapters and agents when they fail.

Therefore, it is up to the client to keep track of state. For example, at a minimum, the client needs to remember **both** the next sequence number to know what data to retrieve next as well as the instanceID in case the agent goes down.

Agent failure is the more complex scenario and requires the use of the instanceId.

The instanceId was created to facilitate recovery when the Agent fails and the application is unaware. Since HTTP is a connectionless protocol, there is no way for the application to easily detect that the agent has restarted, the buffer has been lost, and the sequence number has been reset.

MTConnect Sequence Number

The MTConnect sequence number is between 1 and 18,446,744,073,709,551,615. MTConnect is a RESTful protocol and it is up to the application developer to track the sequence number.

Below is a snippet from running the following simple MTConnect command that runs a sample with a count of 10.

http://agent.mtconnect.org/sample?count=10
```
<Header creationTime="2012-12-26T13:55:15Z" sender="mtconnect"
instanceId="1340212647" version="1.2.0.10" bufferSize="131072"
nextSequence="2933744389"
firstSequence="2933744379"
lastSequence="2933875450"/>
<Streams><DeviceStream name="VMC-3Axis" uuid="000">
```

Notice the bold XML attributes highlighted above in the header. As a developer of applications, the instanceId is important. As was just pointed out in a previous section, the instanceId was created to facilitate recovery when the agent fails and the application is unaware. It is up to the developer to track sequence numbers. Version is important as there have been changes in the standard. The MTConnect specification is the best place to review these changes.

Please note that if you would like to simply cut-and-paste these commands into a browser you can go to http://ToMeasureIsToKnow.com where I have all of these examples listed.

The figure below has the abbreviation of .xsd which stands for XML Schema Definition.

MTConnectDevices_1.2.xsd

```
<xs:element name='MTConnectStreams'
type='MTConnectStreamsType'>
  <xs:annotation>
    <xs:documentation>
    The root node for MTConnect
    </xs:documentation>
  </xs:annotation>
 </xs:element>
 <xs:simpleType name='SenderType'>
  <xs:annotation>
    <xs:documentation>


The date and time the document was created
    </xs:documentation>
  </xs:annotation>
  <xs:restriction base='xs:dateTime'/>
 </xs:simpleType>
 <xs:simpleType name='SequenceType'>
  <xs:annotation>
    <xs:documentation>
    A sequence number
```

```
    </xs:documentation>
   </xs:annotation>
   <xs:restriction base='xs:integer'>
     <xs:minInclusive value='1'/>
     <xs:maxExclusive value='18446744073709551615'/>
```

Notice that in the last three lines we are defining the MTConnect sequence number, which is an integer as well as what the minimum sequence maximum numbers can be.

Four Kinds of MTConnect Responses

It is very important to understand the kinds of MTConnect responses. By responses, this is what is returned from an MTConnect-enabled client. There are four kinds of XML responses in MTConnect. They include devices, streams, assets, and errors.

- **Devices.** Descriptive information about the configuration of the machine(s) and what data can be delivered that are returned by a probe command issued to the agent.

- **Streams.** Data samples and events from the device(s) that are returned by sample or current command issued to agent.

- **Errors.** These are returned when an error occurs that prevents further processing. *Caveat:* most things that don't work as you expect aren't necessarily errors.

- **Assets.** These retrieve information on mobile assets.

To be MTConnect-compliant the device only needs to report on availability.

```
<DataItem category="EVENT" id="avail" type="AVAILABILITY"/>
```

Everything else is optional. Let me repeat this, everything else is optional. The reason for doing this is to allow flexibility with the MTConnect standard.

162

Devices

An agent represents one or more devices. A device (machine) is a collection of components. A component can have subcomponents, allowing representation of arbitrarily complex devices. In fact, the device itself is one type of component.

There's a fixed set of component types. Special components can be used to extend the specification. Each component also has a name, and possibly some other attributes. Here are some examples of the anatomy of a component:

- **Attributes**
  - **UUID.** A globally unique id for the component (required for a device; optional for other component types)
  - **Name.** The name of the component
  - **SampleRate.** An optional sample rate
- **Description**
  - **Example.** Manufacturer, serial number, free-form descriptive text
- **Components.** Subcomponents (recursively defined)
  - A component may have its own data
  - Example: PATH_FEEDRATE for Axes component, in addition to POSITION or ROTARY_VELOCITY for each axis
- **DataItems**
  - What can be reported by this component

The type of data item specifies what (kinds of) values its corresponding samples or events may take.

- POSITION is a numerical value

- EXECUTION is one of IDLE, PAUSED, EXECUTING

- DIRECTION is one of CLOCKWISE or COUNTER_CLOCKWISE

Legal units are codified in the MTConnect Specification.

Streams

A stream is a collection of samples and events organized by device and component. A flat stream of data reduces duplication of static relationships and information, and it can always reference back to devices.

A stream provides simple structure for XML parsing allowing data to be easily aggregated. The probe command returns information on devices which is also known as metadata. The current and sample commands return streams (data). There are two variants of current and one variant of sample.

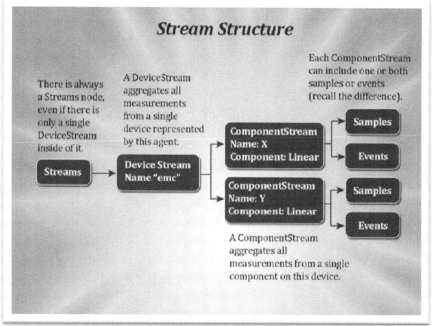

— Created by Will Sobel of System Insights for the MTConnect Institute

Figure 19. *Stream Structure.*

Errors

An error is returned when an error occurs that prevents further processing. Software application developers need to properly handle errors and not let these cause unforeseen results in their applications. This is very basic software developer blocking and tackling.

Assets

An example of an asset is something that is associated with the manufacturing process that is NOT a component of the device *and* can be removed. Remember that a component is a physical entity. Assets are in Part 4 of the MTConnect standard which covers the modeling of these assets and the management and communication of asset data using MTConnect.

Consider these concrete examples of assets:

- Cutting tools, workholding systems, and fixtures

- ISO 13399 standard for describing product data regarding cutting tools, independent from any particular system

- Parts are example of a *future* possibility for assets

- The possibility exists to retrieve information such as (but not limited to) Part ID, description, customer ID, revision ID, process step ID, tooling, target device, program name, revision ID, checksum, target execution time

- Anything where a request could be handled to retrieve information that is not always connected (and therefore mobile) to the particular piece of manufacturing equipment.

The important point to remember on mobile assets for MTConnect is that this is a framework that allows the application to reach out beyond the manufacturing equipment's components and data items that are always connected to that manufacturing equipment.

MTConnect stores assets in a separate "bucket" buffer. The agent provides a limited number of assets that can be stored at one time and uses the same method of pushing out the oldest asset when the buffer is full. The buffer size for the asset storage is maintained separately from the sample, event, and condition storage.

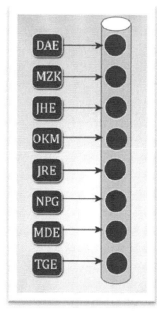

Figure 20. *MTConnect Agent Asset Buffer.*

Assets behave like a key/value in memory database. In the case of the asset the key is the assetID and the value is the XML describing the asset. The key can be any string of letters, punctuation, or digits and represent the domain-specific coding scheme for their assets. Each asset type will have a recommended way to construct a unique assetID, for example, a Cutting Tool *should* be identified by the tool ID and serial number as a composed synthetic identifier.

When an asset is added or modified, an AssetChanged event will be sent to inform us that new asset data is available. The application can request the new asset data from the device. The tool data must remain constant until the AssetChanged event is sent. Once it is sent, data must change to reflect the new content at that instant. The time reflects the time the last change was made to the asset data.

Every time an asset is modified or added it will be moved to the end of the buffer and become the newest asset. As the buffer fills up, the oldest asset will be pushed out and its information removed. The application is responsible for persistence.

For all assets in the agent, request: http://agent.mtconnect.org/assets

This will return all available MTConnect assets in the agent. MTConnect may return a limited set if there are too many asset records. The assets must be added to the beginning with the most recently modified assets. Here's an example url:

http://DavesMachineTool.DE.com/asset/decut1;decut2. Note decut1 and decut2 are mobile asset identifiers.

The following is from github and an example of what might be returned from an MTConnect asset probe.

```xml
<?xml version="1.0" encoding="UTF-8"?>
<!--Sample XML file generated by XMLSpy v2010 rel. 2
(http://www.altova.com)-->
<MTConnectAssets
xsi:schemaLocation="urn:mtconnect.org:MTConnectAssets:1.2
../MTConnectAssets_1.2.xsd"
xmlns:xsi="http://www.w3.org/2001/XMLSchema-instance"
xmlns="uurn:mtconnect.org:MTConnectAssets:1.2"
xmlns:mt="urn:mtconnect.org:MTConnectAssets:1.2">
        <Header creationTime="2001-12-17T09:30:47Z" instanceId="1"
sender="String" version="1.1" bufferSize="112321"/>
        <Assets>
        <ToolAssembly name="MC20006L" serialNumber="112233">
        <Description>0.5000" Drill, HSK63A-ER32 Collet Chuck, 6.000"
Proj</Description>
        <ToolState>FRESH</ToolState>
                <PotCount>1</PotCount>
                <Inserts>
                        <Insert insertId="1">
                        <Length maximum="6.5000" type="NOMINAL"
minimum="5.5000">6.0000</Length>
                        <Diameter maximum="2.0005" type="NOMINAL"
minimum="1.9995">2.0000</Diameter>
                        <TipAngle maximum="90" type="NOMINAL"
minimum="88">90</TipAngle>
                        <CornerRadius maximum="0.0012"
type="NOMINAL" minimum="0.0008">0.0010</CornerRadius>
                        </Insert>
                </Inserts>
        </ToolAssembly>
        <ToolAssembly name="MC2000L"
serialNumber="11233">
                <Description>0.5000" Drill, HSK63A-ER32 Collet Chuck,
6.000" Proj</Description>
                <ToolState>FRESH</ToolState>
                        <PotCount>1</PotCount>
                        <Inserts>
```

```
          <Insert insertId="1">
            <Length type="MEASURED">6.0375</
              Length>
            <Diameter type="MEASURED">
              2.0002</Diameter>
            <TipAngle type="MEASURED">89</
              TipAngle>
            <CornerRadius type="MEASURED">
              0.0011</CornerRadius>
          </Insert>
            <Insert insertId="3">
            <Length type="MEASURED">5.9764</
              Length>
            <Diameter type="MEASURED">
              1.9998</Diameter>
            <TipAngle type="MEASURED">88.5</
              TipAngle>
            <CornerRadius type="MEASURED">
              0.0009</CornerRadius>
            </Insert>
          </Inserts>
        </ToolAssembly>
      </MobileAssets>
</MTConnectAssets>
```

Your First MTConnect Hello World Application

Below is the simplest of Java programs. The program uses Java's basic networking and Input/Output (IO) classes to read agent.MTConnect.org with a probe command. Print the XML out until there is nothing left to print. "Corvette:" is my prompt on my MacBook Pro in a terminal window. Remember you can go to http://ToMeasureIsToKnow.com if you just want to simply cut-and-paste the source code below into your editor or IDE.

Corvette: more MTConnectHelloWorld.java

```
import java.net.*;
import java.io.*;
```

```
public class MTConnectHelloWorld {

        public static void main(String[] args) throws Exception {

          System.out.println("Your First Hello World Program" + "\n");

          URL MTConnect = new URL("http://agent.MTConnect.org/
probe");
          BufferedReader in = new BufferedReader(
          new InputStreamReader(MTConnect.openStream()));

          String inputLine;
          while ((inputLine = in.readLine()) != null)
           System.out.println(inputLine);
          in.close();

          System.out.println("\n" + "XML from probe command printed
above");

     }
}
```

Compile the Java source
Corvette: javac MTConnectHelloWorld.java

Execute the Java class
Corvette: java MTConnectHelloWorld

At this point you will see a few pages of XML coming from the simulator that is running as a CNC vertical mill doing a very simple part in an endless loop.

If you are on a *nix (Mac OS X is obviously in this category as well) box, then you can accomplish the same as above from a command line:

Corvette: curl http://agent.MTConnect.org/probe

If you are a PC user, curl (Command URL) comes with the PowerShell terminal or you could FTP curl as well. As pointed out earlier, you could also do this from a web browser by just putting in the URL http://agent.MTConnect.org/probe. You can put these in your browser to see the results.

Demo.MTConnect.org

The most popular demo that we show at events, such as in the ETC for an IMTS and other manufacturing trade shows, is the device and application MTConnect demo that we make available year around at MTConnect.org This demo is very important because it shows the true genius of MTConnect in a very simple and compelling fashion. This demo is available on the Internet today by going to Demo.MTConnect.org and by selecting a device a shop floor monitoring software application.

Figures 21 and 22 show two screens with devices and applications. The demo is extremely simple, yet very powerful. The key point is that the list of devices is decoupled from the list of applications. It used to be that with a shop floor monitoring and the devices were absolutely tightly locked together with a proprietary protocol. This meant it was impossible to have a variety of shop floor monitoring software packages talk to your shop floor, unless you went and installed a proprietary connection for each and every shop floor monitoring package. Here is a good analogy for this situation. You buy a new house and they ask you what voltage, amperage, and frequency you want for AC power outlets. They ask you this question because there is no standard. You look around you see that some of the lamps you like from Billy-Bob's Lightning and Electric Appliance Supply Company are 190 volt, 7amp and 145 Hz with a four prong proprietary connector. You buy the lamps you like and then you see a really nice toaster, but it turns out that Billy-Bob does not sell any toasters. You find a toaster you like, but it is 120 volts, 15 amps, and 60 Hz. Billy-Bob is glad to sell you his converter from 190 volt, 7amp, and 145 Hz with a four prong proprietary connector to a receptacle that is 120 volts, 15 amps, and 60 Hz. This situation was the exact reason why it was so difficult to connect manufacturing equipment to software applications prior to MTConnect.

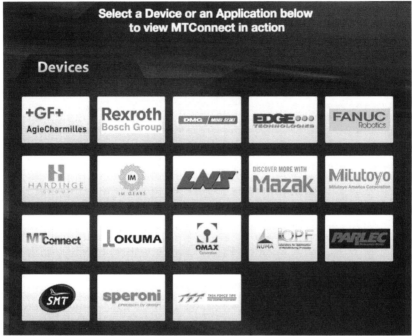

Figure 21. *Demo.MTConnect.org.*

Figure 22. *Demo.MTConnect.org.*

The beauty of the demo is that you can select any device from the top window and any application from the bottom window. All of the devices speak MTConnect as well as all of the software applications speak MTConnect. The user can simply select any device to learn more about it, as well as select any application to speak to the list of devices on the upper part of the demo. The only thing the software applications know about the devices is their name and that they speak MTConnect. This means you can have MTConnect installed once on your manufacturing equipment, such as machine tools, and then try out any of the many MTConnect enabled shop floor monitoring solutions. In this example, MTConnect acts the same as having the standard electrical outlets, so you just need to make sure your appliances have a standard plug on them and you have a world of appliances to choose from.

MTConnect Requests and Responses

As a software developer for MTConnect applications, you need to know how to send the appropriate MTConnect commands to the agent; parse the results; analyze, display, and likely store the returned XML. MTConnect responses are the high-level sections of an MTConnect application. I use the phrase "likely storing," but if you are writing an application, such as shop floor monitoring, I cannot think of a reason why you would **not** be storing the returned data.

It is important to remember the MTConnect big picture:

1. Agent(s) and adapter(s) (adapters are optional) start up.

2. Applications start up and (optionally) query name server to discover agent(s).

    – Application may already know where agent(s) are, e.g., in a relatively static deployment scenario.

3. Applications communicate requests to agents (via HTTP) and receive responses (in XML).

Typically, the first command is a probe to the agent to retrieve the metadata the manufacturing device is capable of providing. The reason to do this is to determine what components and what DataItems this particular piece of manufacturing is capable of providing.

http://agent.mtconnect.org/probe

Run the MTConnect probe command in a browser and notice the devices. We have already discussed the header earlier. Below is a snippet from the probe to show you the devices node, the device with the id of "dev" and the DataItems with the category of "event."

```
<Devices>
    <Device id="dev" iso841Class="6" name="VMC3Axis"
    sampleRate="10" uuid="000">
        <Description manufacturer="SystemInsights"/>
            <DataItems>
                    <DataItem category="EVENT" id="avail"
type="AVAILABILITY"/>
                    <DataItem category="EVENT"
id="dev_asset_chg" type="ASSET_CHANGED"/>
        </DataItems>
```

Notice below the components, the axes, and the DataItems.

```
<Components>
    <Axes id="ax" name="Axes">
        <Components>
                <Rotary id="c1" name="C">
                <DataItems>
<DataItem category="SAMPLE" id="c2" name="Sspeed"
nativeUnits="REVOLUTION/MINUTE" subType="ACTUAL"
type="SPINDLE_SPEED" units="REVOLUTION/MINUTE">

                <Source>spindle_speed</Source>
```

```
        </DataItem>

<DataItem category="SAMPLE" id="c3" name="Sovr"
nativeUnits="PERCENT" subType="OVERRIDE"
type="SPINDLE_SPEED" units="PERCENT">

            <Source>SspeedOvr</Source>
        </DataItem>
        <DataItem category="EVENT" id="cm" name="Cmode"
type="ROTARY_MODE">
            <Constraints>
                    <Value>SPINDLE</Value>
            </Constraints>
        </DataItem>
    <DataItem category="CONDITION" id="Cloadc" type="LOAD"/>
    </DataItems>
</Rotary>
```

http://agent.mtconnect.org/current

The **current** request must return most current components' data values unless the optional at argument is used.

- **at**—[optional] specifying the MTConnect protocol sequence number. Must not be used with the interval command as this will just keep returning the same data repeatedly

Run the MTConnect current command in a browser and notice the devices. We have already discussed the header earlier. Below is a snippet from the current request to show you Streams node, the DeviceStream, the ComponentStream with the id of "Rotary" and the various dataItemIds.

```
<Streams>
        <DeviceStream name="VMC-3Axis" uuid="000">
                <ComponentStream component="Rotary" name="C"
componentId="c1">
                <Samples>
```

175

```
                    <SpindleSpeed dataItemId="c2"
timestamp="2013-01-01T19:34:04.446894Z" name="Sspeed"
sequence="2934360162" subType="ACTUAL">UNAVAILABLE
                    </SpindleSpeed>
                    <SpindleSpeed dataItemId="c3"
timestamp="2013-01-01T19:34:04.446894Z" name="Sovr"
sequence="2934360163" subType="OVERRIDE">UNAVAILABLE<
                    /SpindleSpeed>
            </Samples>
      <Events>
                    <RotaryMode dataItemId="cm" timestamp="2012-06
20T17:17:27.439360Z" name="Cmode"
sequence="16">SPINDLE</RotaryMode>
            </Events>
                    <Condition>
                    <Unavailable dataItemId="Cloadc"
timestamp="2013-01-01T19:34:04.446894Z" sequence="2934360155"
type="LOAD"/>
                    </Condition>
            </ComponentStream>
<ComponentStream component="Controller" name="controller"
componentId="cn1">
      <Events>
                    <EmergencyStop dataItemId="estop" timestamp="2013-
01-01T19:34:04.446894Z"
sequence="2934360171">UNAVAILABLE</EmergencyStop>
                    <Message dataItemId="msg" timestamp="2012-06-
20T17:17:27.439360Z" sequence="28">UNAVAILABLE</Message>
            </Events>
            <Condition>
                    <Unavailable dataItemId="clp" timestamp="2013-01-
01T19:34:04.446894Z" sequence="2934360165"
type="LOGIC_PROGRAM"/>
            </Condition>
```

The sample command retrieves a series of data starting from a position and returns up to the requested number of samples or events. It allows the application to retrieve all data without missing anything. It can stream data as it arrives and be thought of as a window into the stream of data.

The sample request retrieves values for a component's data items.

- **Path**. Xpath expression specifies components and/or data items

  - Default is all components in device or devices if no device is specified

- **From**. Starting sequence number for events, samples, and conditions

  - Default is 0

- **Interval**. Time in milliseconds that the agent should pause between sending samples for events, samples, and conditions

  - Sample can be used with an interval in special cases and this should only be done judiciously (app beware). The interval used to be limited to a minimum of 10 ms, but with the device integration we allowed it to go down to 0.

  - When you specify an interval of zero you're telling the agent that when a value changes, notify me *immediately* and don't try to collect any additional data items. This is great for processes that need to do real-time monitoring (< 10ms). It should always be used with a path since this will allow only specific events to trigger. Real-time is like beauty, it is in the eye of the beholder, so do not think <10ms is a universal definition, it is not, and the definition is absolutely context sensitive.

  - We usually use 1,000 (or one second) intervals between samples.

- **Count.** Must return next sequence

  - Default is 100

Run the following MTConnect sample command in a browser—http://agent.mtconnect.org/sample

Below is a snippet from the sample request (with no additional parameters) to show you the streams node; the ComponentStream; the ComponentStream with the name of "VMC-3Axis"; and the various events, conditions, and data items.

```
<Streams>
        <DeviceStream name="VMC-3Axis" uuid="000">
                <ComponentStream component="Rotary" name="C"
componentId="c1">
        <Samples>


<ComponentStream component="Controller" name="controller"
componentId="cn1">
        <Events>
                <EmergencyStop dataItemId="estop" timestamp="2012-
12-31T04:12:51.242511Z"
sequence="2934232704">UNAVAILABLE</EmergencyStop>
        </Events>
    <Condition>
        <Unavailable dataItemId="clp" timestamp="2012-12-
31T04:11:51.227979Z" sequence="2934232644"
type="LOGIC_PROGRAM"/>
    </Condition>
</ComponentStream>
```

Sampling and XPath

Remember, the path parameter in the command refers to the component structure (not the stream structure). XPath allows arbitrarily complex expressions. Expertise in XPath is always important with web applications that use XML documents and it is certainly the case with MTConnect. If you are not proficient with XPath, you better go brush up on your XPath skills. W3Schools.com has a nice tutorial for XPath.

Let's try a simple XPath expression with the sample request: http://agent.mtconnect.org/sample?count=1000

Everything after the **?** is a parameter passed to the sample command. The above request passes the variable count of 1000. The time range of information received is a function of the sampling rate that the adapter passes to the agent. In the example above at agent.MTConnect.org, the sampling rate is 1,000 samples per second so it is one second of data. This can be verified by looking at nextSequence value of "2934239**884**" and the firstSequence being "2934238**884**. Please note that the numbers you see in bold do not appear that way in the XML output and I do that just so it is easy for the reader to see where the change occurs if you are pulling down one second worth of data.

```
<Header creationTime="2013-01-01T22:35:07Z" sender="mtconnect"
instanceId="1340212647" version="1.2.0.10" bufferSize="131072"
nextSequence="2934239884"
firstSequence="2934238884"lastSequence="2934369955"/>
```

As with most web programming with XML documents, path and // are used as a wildcard and used quite a bit with complicated XML documents.

Run the MTConnect sample command with the wildcard for all Axes in a browser.

http://agent.mtconnect.org/current?path=//Axes

The MTConnect XML response will list Rotary and Linear axes.

```
<ComponentStream component="Rotary" name="C" componentId="c1">
...
<ComponentStream component="Linear" name="X" componentId="x1">
...
<ComponentStream component="Linear" name="Y" componentId="y1">
...
<ComponentStream component="Linear" name="Z" componentId="z1">
```

As would be expected, rotary, X, Y, and Z linear axes information would be returned.

Run the MTConnect sample command with the wildcard for Linear in a browser.

http://agent.mtconnect.org/sample?&path=//Linear

Below are two lines from the response where the component "Linear" was selected.

```
<ComponentStream component="Linear" name="X"
componentId="x1"><Samples>
....
<ComponentStream component="Linear" name="Y"
componentId="y1"><Samples>
.....
<ComponentStream component="Linear" name="Z"
componentId="z1"><Samples>
```

The @ with square brackets [ ] are used to access attributes. This is used to access XML attributes and is used in many MTConnect client applications.

Run the MTConnect sample command in a browser with the wildcard for Linear and look for "X" which would be the X axis. Note the use of single and not double quotes for the X axis.

http://agent.mtconnect.org/sample?&path=//Linear[@name='X']

```
<ComponentStream component="Linear" name="X" componentId="x1">
        <Samples>
                <Position dataItemId="x2" timestamp="2012-12-
31T08:05:24.880333Z" name="Xact" sequence="2934245264"
subType="ACTUAL">UNAVAILABLE
</Position>
        ........
</Samples>
        <Condition>
                <Unavailable dataItemId="Xloadc" timestamp="2012-12-
31T08:05:54.887601Z" sequence="2934245273" type="LOAD"/>
```

```
.........
        </Condition>
</ComponentStream>
```

Run the MTConnect current command in a browser with the wildcard for axes, linear, and DataItem and look for any DataItem that would have an attribute of type=ACTUAL.

```
http://localhost:5000/current?path=//Axes//Linear//DataItem[@subType='
ACTUAL']

ComponentStream component="Linear" name="X" componentId="x1">
        <Samples>
                <Position dataItemId="x2" timestamp="2013-01-
02T01:27:50.765651" name="Xact" sequence="323382"
subType="ACTUAL">-1.3000440598
                </Position>
        </Samples>
</ComponentStream>
<ComponentStream component="Linear" name="Y" componentId="y1">
        <Samples>
                <Position dataItemId="y2" timestamp="2013-01-
02T01:27:50.765651" name="Yact" sequence="323383"
subType="ACTUAL">0.1999527365
                </Position>
        </Samples>
</ComponentStream>

<ComponentStream component="Linear" name="Z" componentId="z1">
        <Samples>
                <Position dataItemId="z2" timestamp="2013-01-
02T01:25:16.123716" name="Zact" sequence="280371"
subType="ACTUAL">-0.1000000015
                </Position>
        </Samples>
 </ComponentStream>

</DeviceStream>
```

Mobile Devices—SAX and DOM Parsing

Joel Neidig who is a systems engineer at ITAMCO wrote the first MTConnect mobile app. He wrote a mobile MTConnect app for both iOS and Android. I created a half-hour webinar under the umbrella of the Offices of Strategic Innovation Roundtable (OSI/R) where I interviewed Joel. This ITAMCO OSI/R is located here http://tinyurl.com/ITAMCO-MTConnect.

Figure 23. *ITAMCO's MTConnect App on an iPhone.*

In this webinar we discuss the exact steps we went through to write a mobile app for MTConnect. Joel discusses Apple's Software Development Kit (SDK) and the steps a developer goes through to write and place an app in the iTunes store. Joel discusses Objective-C and the GUI that is part of the Apple SDK. Joel also discussed Android as well. For Android, Joel used Eclipse as the Integrated Development Environment (IDE). Google has lots of tutorials on how to get started as does Apple.

When I asked Joel what he thought was the trickiest part of developing in iOS, he replied that it was the lack of XML parsers with the SDK. ITAMCO created a Simple API for XML (SAX) parser for iOS. For the Android platform, ITAMCO used a Document Object Model (DOM) parser. DOM on the Android takes more horsepower to run. As this is written for software developers, there are other XML parsing choices and it is not appropriate to discuss this here in further detail. ITAMCO has open sourced both of these apps as well. ITAMCO has since written an MTConnect Blackberry app as well.

At [MC]² 2011, Joel and I had a hands-on session on MTConnect architecture where we go through basic application development with Chris Tacke leading a hands-on

MTConnect Hello World lab as well as Nat Frampton who led a hands-on lab for adapters. The specifics are in the next section.

Running the MTConnect Simulator

There is often a good reason to have your own agent and your own simulator running for testing MTConnect. Below is how to do it with VMware using Linux. Note that the source code is out at github under MTConnect under the cppagent directory. This section assumes you have basic knowledge of Linux.

The overall key to this simulator is that both the simulator and the agent must be running for this to work and you must have an Internet connection even if you are running the simulator. For the agent you will still need access to .xsd file at MTConnect.org.

I documented all of this at my blog and you can see it here and get all of the source code that is needed as well here at: http://tinyurl.com/MTConnectSimulator.

I also include all of the details regarding VMware networking information at my blog.

You can install the simulator and the agent anywhere you like. If you want to set up an ubuntu tiny instance you will need the following pieces from aptget:

1. gcc
2. ruby (had to do an apt-get in order to load this)
3. cmake
4. libxml2
5. libxml2-dev (had to do an apt-get in order to load this)
6. cppunit

Create a directory for the build. Note that you will need to get libxml2-dev.

```
apt-get install ruby
apt-get install libxml2 (likely will tell you that it is installed
apt-get install libxml2-dev
apt-get update
```

ubuntu: /MTConnect_Agent_Simulator_DIR# history |grep apt

```
  1    12:03    apt-get install libxml2
  2    12:04    apt-get update
  4    12:05    apt-cache search libxml
  5    12:05    apt-cache search libxml2
  6    12:13    apt-get install libxml2-dev
 98    13:03    history | grep apt
```

Run the command cmake as indicated below.

```
#cmake -i
```

> * NOTE: just doing regular cmake—if you just keep hitting return on the questions, it will do a proper cmake

> * run this as root

Run the command make as indicated below.

```
# make
```

Now you can run the simulator using the ruby run_scenario.rb script. There is help built in to the script. The default agent.cfg will also startup using the VMC3Axis.xml devices file and the VMC3Axis-Log.txt file will give you the same scenario as we have on the site. Other scenarios can be run by capturing the adapter output into a file and then using that file as the input to be executed by the simulator.

I created the agent and simulator for both Windows and for Linux. I did this for a lab I was teaching in Taipei. I was concerned about my MacBook Pro and the ability to handle a number of students while I was over there, so I asked the man himself, Will Sobel, MTConnect Chief Architect. Will told me,

"40 students could hit the agent and the simulator on my MacBook Pro and probably 100 if you had to."

Directory of /MTConnect_Agent_Simulator_DIR

agent   BUILD.TXT   CMakeFiles   lib

README.md   simulator unix
agent_startup_DIR   ChangeLog   cmake_install.cmake

LICENSE.TXT README.pdf   test   win32
assets   CMakeCache.txt   CMakeLists.txt   Makefile
samples   tools

Directory of
MTConnect_Agent_Simulator_DIR/agent_startup_DIR#

agent agent.cfg

Contents of agent.cfg

```
Devices = ../simulator/VMC-3Axis.xml
AllowPut = true
ReconnectInterval = 1000

Adapters {
  VMC-3Axis {
    Host = localhost
    Port = 7878
            }
        }

# Logger Configuration
logger_config
{
  logging_level = debug
  output = cout
}
```

Because listing agent.sh would take up too many pages of this book, please go to the link http://tinyurl.com/MTConnectSimulator that documents everything that is here for the simulator as well all of the lines of the agent.sh

Below is the startup of the agent in debug mode and below the command is the output you will see.

```
# ./agent debug
```

```
MTConnect Agent Version 1.2.0.14 - built on Mon Jul 30 09:41:08 2012
2012-07-30T15:57:01.307850Z: INFO [0] init.config: Starting agent on
port 5000
2012-07-30T15:57:01.317817Z: INFO [0] init.config: Adding adapter for
VMC-3Axis on localhost:7878
2012-07-30T15:57:01.318606Z: DEBUG [1] input.connector: Connecting
to data source: localhost on port: 7878
2012-07-30T15:57:01.325697Z: DEBUG [1] input.connector: Sending
initial PING
2012-07-30T15:57:01.362692Z: DEBUG [1] input.connector: Received
PONG, starting heartbeats every 10000ms
```

Below is a listing of the simulator directory:

```
run_scenario.rb simple_scenario_1.txt simulator.rb VMC-3Axis-Log.txt
VMC-3Axis.xml
```

Below is the start up of the simulator using ruby in verbose mode and below the command is the output you will see.

```
# ruby -v run_scenario.rb -l VMC-3Axis-Log.txt
```

```
ruby 1.9.3p194 (2012-04-20 revision 35410) [i686-linux]
Waiting on 0.0.0.0 7878
Client connected
```

In the command above, -v is verbose, run scenario.rb is ruby file to be executed and the -l VMC-3Axis-Log.txt is to run log file that contains the simulator data. You can run the netstat command to see which ports are open with the command netstat -anp | grep "LISTEN" and below the command is the output you will see.

```
# netstat -anp | grep "LISTEN"
```

```
tcp    0    0    127.0.0.1:53     0.0.0.0:*    LISTEN    1328/dnsmasq
tcp    0    0    0.0.0.0:23       0.0.0.0:*    LISTEN    4121/inetd
tcp    0    0    127.0.0.1:631    0.0.0.0:*    LISTEN    595/cupsd
tcp    0    0    0.0.0.0:7878     0.0.0.0:*    LISTEN    3622/ruby
tcp    0    0    0.0.0.0:5000     0.0.0.0:*    LISTEN    3627/agent
tcp6   0    0    :::80            :::*         LISTEN    1024/apache2
tcp6   0    0    ::1:631          :::*         LISTEN    595/cupsd
```

Notice that you see the agent at port 5000 and the simulator is at port 7878. You can verify everything is running fine by typing the following in a browser on your VMware instance of Linux (notice the use of port 5000):

```
http://localhost:5000/
```

You will see output that looks like the following snippet:

```
<MTConnectDevices
xsi:schemaLocation="urn:mtconnect.org:MTConnectDevices:1.2
http://www.mtconnect.org/schemas/MTConnectDevices_1.2.xsd"><Head
er creationTime="2013-03-03T15:39:56Z" sender="ubuntu"
instanceId="1362321014" version="1.2.0.14" assetBufferSize="1024"
assetCount="0" bufferSize="131072"/>
<Devices>
    <Device id="dev" iso841Class="6" name="VMC-3Axis"
    sampleRate="10" uuid="000">
        <Description manufacturer="SystemInsights"/>
            <DataItems>
                <DataItem category="EVENT" id="avail"
                type="AVAILABILITY"/>
                <DataItem category="EVENT" id="dev_asset_chg"
                type="ASSET_CHANGED"/>
            </DataItems>
<Components>
```

To make things a little easier, here are some simple startup scripts in the directory:

```
/MTConnect_Agent_Simulator_DIR/simulator#
```

more start_simulator
```
#!/bin/sh
#
ruby -v run_scenario.rb -l VMC-3Axis-Log.txt
```

start_agent_debug_mode
```
#!/bin/sh
#
#
./agent debug
```

The high level instructions are below where in one terminal window you can start the simulator and in a second window startup the agent.

./start_simulator
```
ruby 1.9.3p194 (2012-04-20 revision 35410) [i686-linux]
Waiting on 0.0.0.0 7878
Client connected
```

./start_agent_debug_mode
```
MTConnect Agent Version 1.2.0.14 - built on Mon Jul 30 09:41:08 2012
2013-01-27T15:57:13.055418Z: INFO [0] init.config: Starting agent on port 5000
2013-01-27T15:57:13.060496Z: INFO [0] init.config: Adding adapter for VMC-3Axis on localhost:7878
2013-01-27T15:57:13.061009Z: DEBUG [1] input.connector: Connecting to data source: localhost on port: 7878
2013-01-27T15:57:13.069044Z: DEBUG [1] input.connector: Sending initial PING
2013-01-27T15:57:13.108968Z: DEBUG [1] input.connector: Received PONG, starting heartbeats every 10000ms
```

Notice the PING to the simulator above and then the PONG it receives back? You have to just love Will Sobel's sense of humor when it comes to low-level heartbeats.

Chapter 11: Hands-On MTConnect Labs

Agent and HelloWorld() MTConnect Labs

This section list the three hands-on labs for software developers and implementers interested in learning how MTConnect works. These labs are at MTConnect.org under the Developer section. These labs were done at [MC]^2 2011. You will need a login at MTConnect.org to view these three labs.

NOTE: If you want to have access to the actual MTConnect standard, schema, development documents, and instructions/guidelines, then you simply need to go to MTConnect.org and create a free account very easily.

Once you log in, you will be able to find the three videos I list below that are one hour and 45 minutes each that will answer software developer's basic questions on MTConnect. This starts out with a presentation of the basic MTConnect protocol, shows how to build a reference adapter, and how the agent works as well as writing your first MTConnect application.

- *MTConnect 101: Fundamentals of MTConnect Workshop*
  - Joel Neidig, systems engineer, ITAMCO, and Dave Edstrom of Virtual Photons Electrons

- *MTConnect Architecture: Understanding and Building MTConnect Agents and Adapters Workshop*
  - Nat Frampton, president, Real Time Development Corporation

- *MTConnect Hello World: Building Your First MTConnect Application Using the SDK Workshop*
  - Chris Tacke, president, OpenNetCF Consulting

Hands-On Architecture and Adapter MTConnect Labs

This section list the three hands-on labs for software developers and implementers interested in learning how MTConnect works with specific emphasis on adapters. These labs were done at [MC]² 2013. The plan is to get these on MTConnect.org just like the three labs listed in the previous section. You will need a login at MTConnect.org to view these three labs.

- *MTConnect Architecture Overview*
  - Joel Neidig, systems engineer, ITAMCO
  - Dave Edstrom, president and chairman of the Board MTConnect Institute

- *Adapters, Adapters, Adapters*
  - Will Sobel, president and CEO, System Insights

- *Building Adapters Hands-On Lab*
  - Will Sobel, president and CEO, System Insights

MTConnect-Enabled Client Apps on the Web

There is a brilliant young intern at System Insights, named Prince, who wrote an MTConnect monitoring application called MTConnect graphr that he has open sourced at github. Here is the url to learn more about how Prince created this application at www.tinyurl.com/MTConnectGraphr.

As Prince states in the opening paragraph of his blog post on MTConnectGraphr, "A few months back I took up the fun task of exploring MTConnect streams and the amazing possibilities it presented to a developer. That culminated in a web-based monitoring app, MTConnectGraphr, which can now be downloaded from Github. In this post I'll run down through the development process of the same." This is definitely worth checking out because Prince includes the source and discusses in detail how he built the app.

Running the Agent.exe

Below is the agent command on a Windows PC showing the help command and the parameters that the agent takes:

PS C:\MTConnect1.2\cppagent_win32_1.2.0.13_bin\bin> **./agent help**

MTConnect Agent Version 1.2.0.13 - built on Wed Jun 20 12:23:52 2012

Usage: **agent [help|install|debug|run] [configuration_file]**
    help Prints this message
    install Installs the service
        install with -h will display additional options
    remove Remove the service
    debug Runs the agent on the command line with verbose logging
    run Runs the agent on the command line
    config_file The configuration file to load
        Default: **agent.cfg in current directory**

When the agent is started without any arguments it is assumed it will be running as a service and will begin the service initialization sequence.

Agent.cfg

Below is the agent.cfg on a Windows PC showing default parameters:

PS C:\MTConnect1.2\cppagent_win32_1.2.0.13_bin\bin> **more agent.cfg**

Devices = ../VMC-3Axis.xml
AllowPut = true
ReconnectInterval = 1000
Adapters {
    VMC-3Axis {
        Host = agent.mtconnect.org
Port = 7878
    logger Configuration
logger_config
    logging_level = debug
Output = cout

How to Test Your MTConnect Client

While the MTConnect Institute provides a simulator at http://Agent.MTConnect.org, you could also consider going to github and setting up the MTConnect Simulator yourself. Instead of including all of the information on how to set this up in this document, the reader can go to http://tinyurl.com/MTConnectSimulator to learn how to do this. I have how to setup and use the MTConnect Simulator detailed at the above url.

The Agent Verifier

What if you are creating your own MTConnect agent, how do you verify it is correct? How about a developer who is developing their first MTConnect client application and the developer wants to make sure the agent is correct and responds to MTConnect commands (verbs) in the proper fashion, how do you verify that the MTConnect agent is correct? The answer is the MTConnect agent verifier that Andy Dugenske and the team at Georgia Tech wrote and is at github. The agent verifier will run a variety of tests and will report back those issues to the agent verifier GUI. To change which agent you want to verify, you simple modify the mtcverifier.ini file to select the MTConnect Agent you would like to test.

The agent verifier is a helpful piece of software to have in your arsenal if you are an MTConnect application developer to ensure your agent is acting properly and following the MTConnect standard. The agent verifier is available for free at https://github.com/mtconnect/verifier.

A key point to remember is that you need to have NUnit installed and this can be downloaded for free at http://NUnit.org.

Below is from the documentation for the verifier:

This document describes the Agent Verifier that was built on Microsoft .NET technology which can be used to verify an MTConnect Agent functionality. The MTConnect Verifier uses the NUnit open source unit testing framework for Microsoft .NET using C#. NUnit serves the same purpose as JUnit does in the Java world, and is one of many in the xUnit family.

It is typically recommended that the application architect or analyst write all the unit test cases upfront and test the developed code against these cases and functionalities. The main advantage is a well-defined deliverable and more quantifiable progress.

This may not be applicable if the analyst has already written the MTConnect agent or the analyst has designed the MTConnect agent to be run on other than the Microsoft .NET platform. This issue is resolved by utilizing an external environment (MTConnect Client Application). Think of the MTConnect verifier as an application that checks any MTConnect agent externally similar to the "black box" testing mythology. Since the MTConnect agent uses HTTP this makes external testing very simple.

The MTConnect verifier runs a defined set of test cases against any MTConnect agent that was designed using the MTConnect 1.0 standard. It uses a graphical user interface that indicates the test id, description and a color indicator for pass, fail, or no test.

The MTConnect verifier runs a defined set of test cases against any MTConnect agent that was designed using the MTConnect 1.0 standard. It uses a graphical user interface that indicates the test id, description, and a color indicator for pass, fail, or no test.

The various test cases used in the MTConnect verifier are based on the MTConnect Certification Working Group's documents. The certification documents were divided into eight separate documents based on content sections. The Certification Working Group has defined the certification conformance based on the MTConnect 1.0 standard.

The test cases run on the verifier are divided into the eight certification documents.

The structure of the test cases are named according to the document section and the test case number. Below is the current organization of the certification documents:

Overview of Certification documents

1. *Agent—Certification – General Setup*
2. *Agent—Protocol certification*
3. *Agent—XML Documents certification*
4. *Agent—Devices certification*
5. *Agent—Components certification*
6. *Agent—Data Items certification*
7. *Agent—Streams certification*
8. *Agent—Unit Conversion certification*

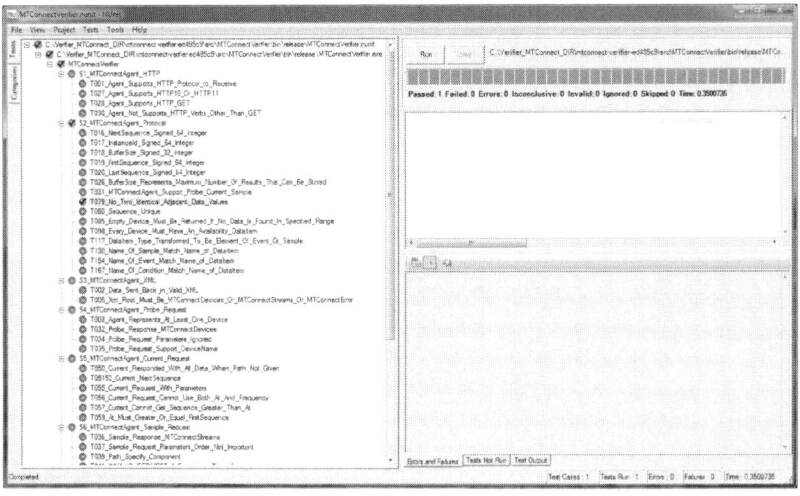

Figure 24. *Screenshot of Agent Verifier.*

Above is a screen shot of the NUnit software with the file MTConnectVerifier.nunit that just passed a single test where it was simply checking for no two identical adjacent data values.

The agent verifier is based on MTConnect 1.0 and .NET. Why would I include it in a book on technology and MTConnect if the software is not current with the standard? Because we have lots of items on our plate at the MTConnect Institute and this would be a great opportunity for an individual or a company, maybe a student even, to take the source code, improve upon it and update for the current standard and then release it back to the world. Go for it!

Security Concerns

The MTConnect agent can be thought of as a simple web server using http. MTConnect is a read-only protocol. As https is not currently supported, there are a variety of ways to provide secure connections. Many users are familiar with setting up a VPN or using SSH to do port forwarding. Specifics of how to do these secure connections are outside the scope of this book, but are easy to find on the Internet. However, I touch on a number of important security points in the Roach Motel section of this book that can be applied here as well.

The reason to provide a secure tunnel for an MTConnect agent is to ensure that data is not being intercepted. While machine tool data might not sound that exciting to steal, imagine if this is for a new medical device and by stealing the data a company could reverse engineer the part. I cannot imagine implementing MTConnect and not putting in a secure tunnel and encrypting all of your data on disk. As I stated earlier, everything in flight (on the network) and at rest (on a disk) should be encrypted. If you do not understand security or vendor does not, hire someone who does.

github

The MTConnect Institute stores its source code at https://github.com/mtconnect. There you will find a great deal of source code and binaries. Most of the source and binaries are for the agent and adapters, but you will see the "cstream" source code at https://github.com/mtconnect/cstream as an example of a simple web request that returns XML that is written in C.

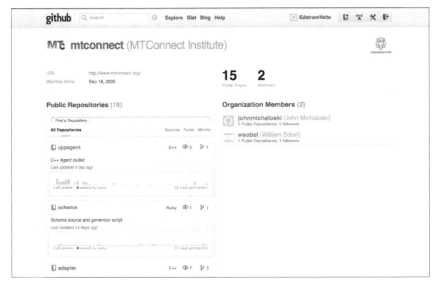

Figure 25. *Where to find MTConnect source code.*

Where to Go for Help

The MTConnect Forum, at http://MTConnectForum.com is the right place to post your MTConnect questions on any MTConnect topic. Specifically for software development, in the Applications section at http://mtconnectforum.com/forum/Forum6.aspx or http://tinyurl.com/MTConnectForumApps.

If you do not get an answer there, drop me a note and I will either respond with the answer or research the question and then reply.

Getting Started With MTConnect Series of White Papers

Connectivity Guide

"Getting Started with MTConnect" is an umbrella term that we use at the MTConnect Institute for educational white papers. The first white paper in this series was led by Dave McPhail, president and CEO of Memex Automation, and John Turner, director of technology for FAC&T. I was very fortunate when I asked both John and Dave and they agreed to lead this very important effort. The *Connectivity Guide* is by far the most popular download at MTConnect.org. This guide addresses the fundamental question, "How do I get started, and what do I need to know and do in my own shop to get MTConnect enabling my manufacturing equipment?"

This guide was put together by an impressive group of industry experts who really understand the variety of devices that can be MTConnect enabled. Below are the 16 companies that collaborated on the initiative.

- Memex Automation, Inc. Co-Chair
- FA Consulting & Technology, LLC Co-Chair
- Advanced Technologies Services, Inc.
- FANUC FA America
- General Dynamics—OTS
- Georgia Tech Factory Information Systems Lab
- Nexas Networks Inc.
- Pinaka Systems, Inc.
- Predator Software, Inc.
- Real Time Development Corp.
- Remmele Engineering, Inc.
- SCADAware, Inc.
- Southern Manufacturing Technologies, Inc.
- System Insights, Inc.
- TechSolve, Inc.
- Virtual Photons Electrons, LLC

The paper details the necessary steps to be successful:

1. Define the problem that you are trying to solve
2. Define what success looks like
3. Define your equipment
4. Define limitations/restraints that impact your project
5. List the people in your organization who will impact the project

I strongly encourage everyone who is interested in MTConnect to read this white paper.

Shop Floor Monitoring, What's in It for You?

The MTConnect Institute is working on a white paper called, "Getting Started with MTConnect: Shop Floor Monitoring, What's in It for You?" Dave McPhail of Memex Automation and I are leading this effort with a small group helping out. I would strongly encourage everyone to go to MTConnect.org to download this white paper. This white paper will be released at [MC]² 2013. Shop floor monitoring will be a big part of [MC]² 2013. Dave McPhail and I are leading a hour and 40 minute panel session on shop floor monitoring that will have customers and executives from shop floor monitoring companies sharing their real life lessons learned with the audience. This video of the panel will be made available at MTConnect.org after [MC]² 2013.

Below are the companies who contributed to this white paper.

- Memex Automation Inc. (Chair)
- General Dynamics – OTS
- Scytec Consulting Inc.
- MacKintok Inc.
- Connecticut Center for Advanced Technology, Inc. (CCAT)
- Task Force Tips

- Remmele Engineering, Inc.
- System Insights, Inc.
- Virtual Photons Electrons, LLC (Co-Chair)

When exploring MTConnect enabling your plant or shop floor, do not fall into the "all or nothing" trap of implementations. What I am referring to is the comment that I from some that say, "if I do not MTConnect enable my entire shop, then what is the point?" As with any project, you want to walk before you run. Decide on three to five machines you want to monitor, get those MTConnect enabled and then go to the many shop floor monitoring solution providers and ask for a trial period to test out their software. The beauty of MTConnect is that once you MTConnect enable these three to five machines, it will be very straightforward to try out different shop floor monitoring solutions because unlike proprietary offerings, you will not have to change the drivers each time – different devices, common connect.

The other trap to avoid is to make sure that perfect does not become enemy of the good as the old adage states. I am referring to the notion that "if I can't monitor every single piece of data on each machine, then why monitor at all?" That logic is just as backwards as thinking you have to start off monitoring every piece of equipment in your shop. Don't try to boil the ocean.

Getting Started With MTConnect: Writing Client Applications

As I mentioned earlier, I have had a number of conversations with my oldest John, who is a gifted software developer at Facebook and was a developer at Microsoft working on Windows 8 security, but he knows nothing about manufacturing. What MTConnect really needs are the John Edstroms of the world developing MTConnect applications. Currently 99.9999 percent of software developers are not in the manufacturing arena, and we need to get them interested and educated. The reason I believe so strongly in this is because manufacturing is absolutely ripe for creative integration through new applications. MTConnect is becoming a huge enabler for manufacturing on the shop floor.

I am in the final stages of writing a white paper called, "Getting Started With MTConnect: Writing Client Applications" which will be at MTConnect.org and will use parts from this book. I expect this white paper to be on MTConnect.org in the early summer 2013 time frame. This white paper will be strictly for software developers, and in particular the huge world of software developers who are not in manufacturing but want to understand how MTConnect works and how to write client applications for MTConnect.

I stated this previously, but it is worth repeating in this section on the topic of domain knowledge. While it is obvious that it would be very helpful to have deep manufacturing domain knowledge, it is not critical for the reader to have *deep* expertise of manufacturing. Deep manufacturing expertise is needed if the reader intends to write an MTConnect agent or adapter. This is not to diminish the value of this domain knowledge, but you don't need machinist experience in order to write an application to get data off a machine tool. In the same way that a software developer does not need to be a neurosurgeon to write a medical application, the same is true of writing MTConnect client applications. However, the software developer does need to have a baseline knowledge of the nature of the business domain and this paper will provide high-level domain overview and pointers to additional documents and resources.

Sustainable Aerospace Manufacturing Initiative

The Connecticut Center for Advanced Technology (CCAT) and National Center for Defense Manufacturing and Machining (NCDMM) have been fantastic supporters of MTConnect in a number of important ways. CCAT and NCDMM supported the creation of a great white paper at MTConnect.org called, "Sustainable Aerospace Manufacturing Initiative" (SAMI) that I strongly recommend individuals read. While this white paper is not part of the, "Getting Started With MTConnect" series of white papers it is an excellent white paper that is certainly worth downloading and reading.

This white paper has the following sections (as taken from the white paper itself) in it:

Section I Components and Elements of Sustainable Aerospace Manufacturing, which discusses the details the measurement tool developed to support the evaluation of technologies relative to the components/elements of Sustainable Manufacturing.

Section II Software Application Review: Which is a review of ten (10) software applications and provides an assessment of how each addresses the components/elements of Sustainable Manufacturing.

Section III MTConnect Specification Evaluation: Which is a review of the MTConnect specification and how it addresses the components/elements of Sustainable Manufacturing.

Section IV Conclusions: Which is a summary of the findings of the project and recommendations for future projects to advance the state of Sustainable Manufacturing.

Summary—Different Devices, Common Connection

When I started consulting for AMT and working for Doug Woods, I told the story of Java at Sun Microsystems. A point that I made was that one of the key aspects of Java was the slogan "Write Once, Run Anywhere" (WORA). This four word description was so clear and succinct that anyone could understand the benefits. A software developer could write their software just once and run it on any platform. Gone were the days of Mac only, PC only, or platform-specific software.

I had asked Doug and others for suggestions on the four words we could use to summarize MTConnect. Many of us shot out a series of suggestions, but none of them had the punch we were looking for until Doug came up with, "Different Devices, Common Connection." I have that phrase on my signature line in MTConnect-related emails because it drives home the point just like WORA does for Java.

Acknowledgements

This One Goes To 11

This is far and away the most difficult section of this book to write. I don't want to forget someone, or have the order that I list individuals somehow diminish their contribution. My upfront apologies if I screwed up and forgot someone or if an MTConnect contributor is offended on the order of names listed below. That is clearly not my intent. I have over 15 pages of acknowledgements, so I gave it my best shot.

Doug Woods is a true visionary for manufacturing and it has been a real privilege working for Doug and consulting to AMT these past three-plus years. I was very fortunate when Doug asked me out to lunch in February 2010 and asked me what I was doing after Sun Microsystems was purchased by Oracle. My plan was to take one year off. I've had a job since I was 16 (for a brief time period I had two jobs and was going to college at night) and I was 50 years old and was going to take a break. I turned down a number of job offers in early 2010. Doug told me that he wanted to get some of my time if I was interested. I put together what I thought would be a win for AMT and a win for Dave Edstrom. I suggested to Doug that I would work for him as a consultant and create the Office of Strategic Innovation (OSI) at AMT working on MTConnect and what would become MT*Insight* as well as some other emerging technology for AMT. Doug has been a great guy to work for. Truth be told, it was not a hard sell as I knew all the folks at AMT were best-of-class individuals and AMT was a proven thought leader among trade associations.

Paul is an absolutely great guy with a million connections in manufacturing. Paul also has a million connections inside government as well. No Paul Warndorf, no MTConnect. I can't say enough good things about Paul. It is absolutely true that Paul has been MTConnect's shepherd, conductor, and guiding light. MTConnect needs to clone Paul Warndorf. If you see Paul Warndorf, you should walk up to him and shake his hand to thank him for everything that he has done for MTConnect and manufacturing around the globe. You should ask Paul, what YOU can do to help in the MTConnect revolution!

John Byrd was and is a real mentor to me. John's vision on MTConnect was perfect from the very beginning. John is an industry icon and thought leader in the global world of manufacturing. John's very famous quote, "MTConnect will be more important in the 21st century for manufacturing than CNC was for manufacturing in the 20th century" has been in 100 percent of every MTConnect presentation I have ever done. I promise you that quote has done more for MTConnect than any other single sentence. I remember flying back from an MTConnect meeting with John back in 2008 where we were discussing MTConnect's future. John was sharing with me during that flight exactly what needed to happen and what it would take for MTConnect to be successful. Five years later John is being proven right every day. I am very fortunate that I can still reach out to John for advice. John is moving to Chicago, but I am hopeful we can still keep in touch.

Will Sobel is the chief architect of MTConnect and president of System Insights. Will built MTConnect. Yes, many others helped, but Will Sobel is on the MTConnect Mount Rushmore. He is a brilliant programmer who works tirelessly on every aspect of MTConnect ranging from the standard all way through the source code for the agent, adapters, simulators, applications, you name it. If you go out to github in the MTConnect section for both source code and binaries you will see one name over and over again—wsobel. That is because Will Sobel wrote almost all of the software that we use as reference adapters, the reference agent, and sample applications for MTConnect which other companies and individuals can use as they start off in MTConnect. Will gives of himself in ways that are difficult to appreciate unless you work with him on a regular basis. He is a rare individual indeed. I learn something every time I speak with him.

Peter Eelman first got me involved with AMT in 2000, and as I mentioned earlier, he is a great guy, fantastic neighbor, a real manufacturing industry icon, and a true friend. We share a lot in common including season tickets to the Wizards. We do root for different football teams though.

I mentioned that one of the luckiest days of my life was when Dave Patterson agreed to work with me on MTConnect at the very beginning with our joint keynotes at AMT's Annual Meeting in Lake Las Vegas, Nevada, in October 2006. I cannot thank Dave enough. I also sincerely appreciate the very nice foreword that he wrote in this book. Dave is a legend in the computer industry and it was the thrill of my life to work with him on MTConnect. I would also encourage everyone to contribute to Dave's Waves To Wine effort that he does every year for Multiple Sclerosis (MS). You can google "Waves to Wine" and MS to learn more and make a contribution.

Dr. Armando Fox of University California Berkeley was involved from the very beginning and made many critical contributions to MTConnect.

I am very fortunate to have the most elite group of board members ever assembled. As president and chairman of the board for the MTConnect Institute, I feel like a coach of a professional all-star team. My job is to listen and learn from this world-class group of industry thought leaders, and together we set the course for MTConnect. I have already mentioned Doug Woods and Paul Warndorf, and both of them are on the Board. Brian Papke, president of Mazak USA, has been a tremendous friend and supporter of MTConnect. I have learned countless important lessons from Brian over the years.

The MTConnect Institute and I are very fortunate to have Brian Papke on its board, and I am very fortunate to be able to seek his guidance. When Brian speaks, everyone listens because of the tremendous respect everyone has for Brian Papke. Ralph Resnick, president of the National Center for Defense Manufacturing and Machining, (NCDMM), has been a real friend and supporter of MTConnect. Ralph is also on the Board of Directors of MTConnect. NCDMM is also running the "MTConnect Challenge" which is a fantastic program for manufacturing. I am very fortunate to be able know someone who is such a thought leader as Ralph Resnick. Courtney Hill, formerly of GE Aviation, is on the MTConnect Board of Directors and is one of those brilliant individuals who I could listen to for hours on end because of his very deep and broad expertise. Courtney is also an outstanding speaker, and we are very fortunate to have him at [MC]² 2013. Courtney has the rare ability to synthesize difficult problems into manageable sections so solutions can come about and guide us to not try to boil the ocean. When Courtney was at GE Aviation, he led the group that provided a very generous gift to the MTConnect Institute to help build the standard. Dr. Dean Bartles, vice president Advanced Programs and Strategic Growth for General Dynamics–Ordnance and Tactical Systems, must have three other clones running around because he seems to be able to keep so many balls in the air that he simply cannot be just one person. Dean was one of the first individuals in manufacturing to recognize the value of MTConnect when General Dynamics made a generous gift to the MTConnect Institute. Dean is extremely creative and always sending myself and the MTConnect Board emails with innovative ideas. I should also add that Dr. Bartles will be receiving his second Ph.D. in May of 2013. I joked with Dean, "Do we now have to call you 'Dr. Dr. Bartles?' "

John Turner, Director of Technology for FA Consulting and Technology (FAC&T), is the shepherd for the MTConnect

Standard. He is one of the sharpest and hardest working individuals that I know. John and I touch base every Monday morning to make sure we are on the same page. I learn something from John every time we speak. Every presentation that I do for MTConnect, I mention Turner's Five Laws of Manufacturing. John's four decades in manufacturing is priceless. Plus, he is just a hell of a good guy.

There have been no better friends to MTConnect than the great folks at Gardner Business Media, Inc. (GBMI). Rick Kline, Sr., Rick Kline Jr., Missy Kline Skavlem, Mark Albert, Travis Eagan, and the entire Gardner crew have been incredibly supportive of MTConnect, and the [MC]² conferences. It is impossible to say too many good things about our good friends at Gardner. Mark Albert's passion, expertise, and industry recognition puts him in a very rare class of leaders. Mark's writing ability is something that I truly admire, and I wish I was as gifted in telling the MTConnect story as Mark.

Thanks to Red Heitkamp, Mark Conley, and Bill Blomquist of Remmele Engineering for all of their help, guidance, and support over the years. Thanks to Roy Sweatman, Shannon Sweatman, and Pat Walsh for their guidance on what is best for those individuals that matter the most in MTConnect—the end users or the manufacturers. Their advice and suggestions have been invaluable. The MTConnect Institute teamed National Tooling and Machining Association (NTMA) to create a framework to make it easy for NTMA members to try out MTConnect. Pat, Roy, and Shannon represented NTMA and worked extremely hard for NTMA's members to help their members realize the benefits of MTConnect.

Scott Hibbard, of Bosch Rexroth, has been a tremendous contributor and supporter of MTConnect. Scott has been involved with MTConnect from the very beginning and has personally helped me get smarter about manufacturing. Thanks to Scott, I was able to attend a Bosch Rexroth

"IndraMotion MTX L45/L65 Version 12VRS" and it was an absolutely excellent hands-on course that I would highly recommend for those individuals who want to understand how a CNC really works and how to program it.

Tom Scotton, manager of Modeling and Simulation for the Connecticut Center for Advanced Technology (CCAT) and NCDMM have been fantastic supporters of MTConnect in a number of important ways. CCAT and NCDMM supported the creation of a great white paper at MTConnect Institute called, "Sustainable Aerospace Manufacturing Initiative" (SAMI) that I strongly recommend individuals read. I also had the privilege of speaking at CCAT after Tom hosted an MTCTAG meeting in Hartford, CT, in December of 2012.

Thanks to Tom Burke, president and chairman of the board for the OPC Foundation, for being such a great partner. At IMTS 2010, Tom made the following statement regarding the Memorandum of Understanding between OPC Foundation and the MTConnect Institute, "MTConnect and OPC collaborating will provide the necessary infrastructure to revolutionize interoperability for the complete spectrum of manufacturing technology, by leveraging the standards of both organizations, evolving the technology that has already been well accepted and adopted by the suppliers." I made the following statement for our joint press release, "This is not just a win for MTConnect and OPC, this is a huge step forward for manufacturing interoperability around the globe."

One of the genuine privileges of working in the manufacturing area is when you run into someone that is a true thought leader and a game changer. It is even more inspiring when that person is young. Joel Neidig is a Technology Manager at ITAMCO and is a role model for what we want young people in manufacturing to aim for. Actually, he is a role model for anyone. He was a key contributor for both [MC]² 2011 and [MC]² 2013. The great American computer scientist Alan Kay, who invented SmallTalk and Object Oriented Programming (OOP), once said, "The best way to predict the future is to invent it." Joel is inventing the future at ITAMCO as well as his many contributions to MTConnect. I love to talk to Joel because it gives me a glimpse into where manufacturing is going. Joel is able to predict the future because he is helping to invent it. The future of manufacturing is very bright and very cool. It will be both fun and educational to watch what Joel does next.

Huge thanks to Dave McPhail, president of Memex Automation who has always been there when I have come to him with the huge MTConnect challenges that we have faced over the years. Dave is a great guy and so is his business partner at Memex Automation, John Rattray, who is the vice president of sales and marketing, as well as the whole Memex Automation team. In September of 2010, I came to Memex Automation's booth to ask Dave if he would team with John Turner to work on an incredibly important white paper called, "Getting Started With MTConnect: Connectivity Guide." I needed someone who was well known and well respected in manufacturing and who had a reputation of getting things done. Dave McPhail was the perfect person for the task. He and John Turner led the team and they hit it out of the park in terms of the *Connectivity Guide*. As I mentioned, it is by far the most popular document downloaded at MTConnect.org. This paved new ground, and it required real leadership to make this a reality. Dave also leads the effort for "Getting Started With MTConnect: Shop Floor Monitoring, What's In It For You?" which I am sure will be a great white paper as well. Dave has been a real friend and someone I can turn to for expert and thoughtful advice. Thanks as well to Bob Hansen of R.C. Hansen Consulting for his help at [MC]² 2013 and educating me on OEE. Bob did a great job really creating an excellent presentation on OEE and MTConnect where the theme of his talk was called, "Combining MTConnect with OEE = Intelligence." Most importantly, intelligence can lead to profits. Bob did a great job putting MTConnect and OEE into terms that everyone can understand and appreciate. Thanks to Dave McPhail for introducing me to Bob.

When I think of MTConnect and those individuals who are out there day-in and day-out working with customers and leading the MTConnect charge, I think of Neil Desrosiers. Neil is a recognized technical and business leader at Mazak and in the industry. Neil is a very talented software developer as well which gives him the unique ability to understand all aspects of an MTConnect solution. Neil very well might be the world leader in a number of MTConnect installations he has personally led. I get energized every time I hear what Neil is doing with MTConnect with Mazak's customers. Thanks to Neil Desrosiers of Mazak and Leslie Galbreath of DGS Marketing for allowing me to use photos of Mazak machine tools in this book as well.

Larry Schwartz of Okuma has been a tremendous supporter of MTConnect. I have had the privilege of speaking at a number of Okuma events. Larry sits on AMT's Board of Directors and has been extremely supportive of MTConnect and providing his guidance to the MTConnect Institute. Brian Sides, of Okuma, has been a great supporter of MTConnect and of open systems for manufacturing for a long, long time. Brian has educated me on manufacturing in general and specifically, the history of open systems in manufacturing, such as Okuma's impressive THINC open architecture. Brian has a BS in Computer Engineering and leads a team at Okuma. Okuma was the sponsor of the very nice polo shirts for all [MC]² 2011 and [MC]² 2013 attendees. These [MC]² 2013/Okuma shirts are reason enough to attend an [MC]² conference in my opinion, but I am biased. Thanks as well to Julie Murphy of Okuma for all of her tremendous support of MTConnect. Julie is a real professional. Thanks to Julie Murphy and Brian Sides of Okuma for allowing me to use photos of Okuma machine tools in this book as well.

Ken Tock and Gary Bronson, of MacKintok Information Architects and Designers, have done an outstanding job with the creation of MTConnect.org and MTConnectForum.com. The MTConnect Institute is so fortunate to have a member who is an expert in manufacturing and a world-class web design company as well. We owe a great deal to Ken and Gary for all their help and guidance. Thanks to Hilena Hailu for her great work with the MTConnect Forum and MTConnect.org in guiding the efforts of MacKintok. It is fantastic that AMT was able to hire such a bright and passionate person away from Microsoft to help lead MTConnect. Hopefully Hilena will be at AMT for a long time to take MTConnect to greater heights.

I have had the privilege of speaking at Mori-Seiki Innovation Days in both 2011 and 2012. These are fantastic events that are really customer focused. Sincere thanks to Dana Super and Surya Kommareddy of Mori-Seiki for their MTConnect support over the years. Thanks to Stewart McMillan and Nate Price of Task Force Tips (TFT). TFT is a truly unique and incredibly innovative company and led by movers and shakers who are on the leading-edge of manufacturing.

Thanks to Andy Dugenske of Georgia Tech for his tremendous support of MTConnect over the years. Andy has led numerous efforts to help MTConnect including the MTConnect agent verifier, which is extremely important to MTConnect developers. Plus, Andy is a car guy who I love to discuss sports cars with whenever we are together. Andy is an expert in many areas and the MTConnect Institute is very fortunate to have Georgia Tech and Andy as a partner.

Thanks to our great friends at TechSolve—Ron Pieper and Amit Deshpande. Ron and Amit have been MTConnect thought leaders and supporters for many years now. TechSolve has been a big supporter of MTConnect. Mark Doyle of I/Gear Online was a panel host at [MC]² 2011 and did a great job. Special thanks to Prof. Eraldo Jannone da Silva, School of Engineering, University of Sao Paulo, who has given fantastic presentations at both [MC]² 2011 and [MC]² 2013. We had a number of great hands-on labs at [MC]² 2011 that were led by Nat Frampton of Real Time Development and Chris Tacke of OpenNETCF Consulting

Special thanks to Tony Paine and Kepware Technologies for Kepware's great support over the years. Tony is president and co-owner of Kepware Technologies. Kepware Technologies have supported the MTConnect Institute in a variety of ways including being sponsors and exhibitors at [MC]² 2013. Kepware Technologies is a member of MTConnect, and in 2011 I had the privilege of providing a quote when Kepware announced their KEPServerEX's MTConnect Driver. Kepware Technologies is a great company.

Thanks to Dr. Athulan Vijayaraghavan of System Insights who is one of the smartest, most passionate, and funniest individuals I know. Athulan is the CTO for System Insights and came out of UCB studying under Dr. Dave Dornfeld. Athulan is one of the up-and-coming superstars in manufacturing. Thanks to Pete Tecos and Dan Janka of MAG for their support of MTConnect.

Thanks to Dr. Dave Dornfeld who is chairman of the Department of Mechanical Engineering and the Laboratory for Manufacturing and Sustainability at UC Berkeley. Dave hosted many of the initial MTConnect meetings. Dave received AMT's Charles F. Carter Jr. Advancing Manufacturing Award in March 2012. Dave is a brilliant man with an amazing sense of humor. Once at a conference in Nashville, Dave made a very interesting statement regarding slicing through the data of any presentation. What Dave basically said was, *"anytime you see 40 percent in a presentation you should be suspect. The presenter likely did not want to put in 50 percent because it would be viewed too high and 30 percent would be viewed as not being significant."* I got a real chuckle out of that and said to Dave, "I think we need to call that "Dornfeld's Law," so I did on a blog entry where I stated:

"Dornfeld's Law states that the statistical veracity of any presentation can be quickly determined by examining both the frequency and relative contextual importance of the number 40 percent in the presenters representation of supporting data."

Thanks to Tim Shinbara for educating me on the leading and bleeding edge of manufacturing technology.

Thanks to Chris Nuccitelli of Parlec for all of his support. Thanks as well to Tom Muller of Kennametal. It's always great to see Chris and Tom at MTCTAG meetings or the different manufacturing shows that occur each year. Chris Kaiser of BIG Kaiser has been a real friend and supporter of MTConnect over the years. Don Martin of Lion Precision was the chairman of the Sensor Group and did a fantastic job leading the group. Lion Precision has been a great partner of the MTConnect Institute. Thanks to Rick Caldwell of SCADAware for his support. Rick provides the MTConnect Institute with great insight on very important and pragmatic guidance. Thanks to Randy Lewis of LNS for all of his hard work with MTConnect. Thanks to Rick Mosca of Mind Over Machines who has helped out with MTConnect and MT*Insight*. Thanks to Martin Humphreys of Edge Technologies. Thanks to Yigal Ziv of Lemoine Technologies. Thanks to Jim Abbassian of Predator Software. Thanks to Josh Davids of Scytec for his leadership in a wide variety of efforts and very important white papers. Josh was very involved with the MTConnect Shop Floor Monitoring white paper. Thanks to Tom Gaasenbeek and Jim Smith for their guidance and support of MTConnect.

Sincere thanks to the National Kaohsiung University of Applied Sciences in Taiwan and specifically Dr. Yung-Chou Kao of the Department of Mechanical Engineering and to the Precision Machinery Research & Development Center (PMC) in Taiwan and specifically, Benjamin B. C. Jan, general manager of PMC; Alan Wei, manager of PMC; and Dr. Katie Mei of PMC. Special thanks as well to the young and brilliant employees of PMC—Wyatt Wu, Joseph, Kenny and Terry for all of their help while I was in Taiwan. Words cannot describe how great it was to be in Taiwan. It was the absolute best I have ever been treated in my life! It was an absolute honor to be there and have the chance to discuss MTConnect at a conference and teach a hands-on lab at PMC as well. I gave a three-hour presentation on MTConnect and taught a six-hour hands-on lab discussing every aspect of MTConnect in Taiwan. It was real time converted to Mandarin Chinese as I spoke and taught. PMC is also a sponsor at [MC]² 2013 which is fantastic and greatly appreciated.

Thanks to Beth Groundwater, who is a well-known author, for her guidance. I have had many great managers over the years to thank such as Betsy Ferry, Joy Warfield, Sue Walls, Brad Kirley, Dan Hushon, and James Hollingshead. Thanks to Jeff Stone, Connie Stack, Richard Franklin, Dr. Glen Gawarkiewicz, Mike Groene, Neil Groundwater, Mike O'Dell, Hal Stern, Dr. Dennis Govoni, Neal Thomison, Tim Wallace, Steve Ferry, Roger Fujii, the late Brian Carney, John Morrell, Dr. Bruce Haddon, John Dicarlo, Darren Govoni, Mike Briggs, Jim Caldwell, Tim Smith, Brian Raymor, Joel McClung, and Bob West for their great friendship and advice over the years. I have run countless ideas by them over the many decades, and I have either received great guidance or a RTFM.

MT*Insight* Thanks

Steve Fanning, president of Path To Progress, has been one of the chief architects of MT*Insight* and a database god. I do not use the term database god lightly here either. Steve has been a guiding force behind MT*Insight*. Steve and I worked together very closely to create the architecture for MT*Insight* in early 2010 and through the summer of 2010 as well. Steve has been consulting to AMT since 1979 and AMT is quite fortunate to have Steve available to them. Steve is also recognized as the world's expert on Grand Marnier. I am serious—Google it. Lois Uthman, director of IT for AMT, has been the steady, guiding hand that keeps us looking over the horizon so all the parts keep running extremely well. Lois keeps all of AMT's many IT parts all working extremely well together and has been a key driving force with MT*Insight*. Pat McGibbon, VP of Industry Intelligence for AMT, has been the father and visionary of MT*Insight* and is known as one of the top economists and statisticians in all of manufacturing. Pat is an expert on many topics and has countless connections both inside and outside of manufacturing. Pat McGibbon is just a truly great guy. Julie Peppers (formerly Julie Germain) and Ian Stringer have been involved in MT*Insight* from day one and have really been the driving force with their great passion and intelligence. Julie is the project manager for MT*Insight* and does an outstanding job and seems to have a photographic memory. Ian wears many hats, and his unique ability to think outside that box is something that is truly amazing and I admire. Sinisa Kurtic is a consultant that has saved MT*Insight* on so many occasions that I have lost track. Sinisa is like superman who comes in to save the day. Thanks to Russ Waddell for all of the interesting conversations and creative ideas that he has shared over the years.

A very fortunate day for MT*Insight* was when Actuate assigned Aamir Khwaja and Kalesh Mahendrakar to the AMT account. Aamir was the perfect PS manager, and Kalesh, was and is, a very talented software developer. Kalesh did a great job creating apps for MT*Insight*. Fortunately for AMT, Kalesh has come to work directly for AMT and now is the BI architect for MT*Insight*. Alka Parandekar is a very gifted software developer at AMT who is on the MT*Insight* Development Team and seems to be working 24-hours a day and always is able to not only deliver great products on time, but also provides us with deep and insightful analysis in countless areas. Marnie Douglas is the Actuate sales rep who has been a real partner for MT*Insight*. I can't say enough good things about Marnie's professionalism, follow through, customer care and passion. Special thanks as well to Pete Citadinni, president of Actuate, who has been a real supporter of MT*Insight* and who is a car guy like me. I went out to dinner with Pete, Marnie, and Dave Garnett once, and Pete picked me up in his Fiskar Karma, which was very cool. Thanks to Clement Wong, Steve Cotugno, Brian Moser, and Gautam Goswami of Actuate as well for their help over the years.

AMT is extremely fortunate to have Steve Lesnewich as the leader of the entire MT*Insight* team. Steve has decades of experience leading talented teams and is a true business leader. Mark Kennedy and Kim Brown do a fantastic job in selling and demonstrating MT*Insight* apps and also are the voice of the customer. Mark and Kim are as passionate and smart as any two sales reps on planet earth. Steve, Mark, and Kim provide the voice of the customer for MT*Insight* and their insight is forever changing manufacturing.

Diyana Hrzic, Bonnie Gurney, Michelle Edmonson, and Kate Fritz have all been instrumental in MT*Insight*'s success from the overall website, to communications, to app definitions, and helping members. Diyana provides great insight on the direction of MT*Insight* from both a business and technical perspective. Diyana is also the world's best video editor. Michelle's input and guidance on IMTS is a key reason that app is known as the killer MT*Insight* app. Kate has provided priceless input on a number of apps for MT*Insight* and gives the MT*Insight* a real voice of the member, which is key.

Sincere thanks to Jeff Traver, Malcolm Mason, Mario Winterstein, Knox Johnstone, and Kathy Milks of AMT's Business Development for their deep expertise and guidance on a wide variety of international issues that were all new to me. It was and is greatly appreciated.

Doug Woods has been proven prescient in the direction manufacturing needs to be going. Doug's support of MTConnect, at the absolute very beginning when he was chairman of the board for AMT, was absolutely crucial for MTConnect's success. Doug has hit another home run with his prophetic vision and strong support for MT*Insight* because he knows that the ability to connect to a wide variety of data sources, digest huge amounts of data, analyze, and convey information in a variety of formats will determine the winners and losers in manufacturing going forward. AMT's members, as well as those non-members who are eligible for certain apps, can take advantage of MT*Insight*'s many applications are seeing something that is quite rare for an association and that is honest to god creative and pragmatic leadership that changes how companies do business. I can not think of another trade association that has done more for its members. When Doug Woods walks out the door the last time for AMT, there will be a long list of very impressive accomplishments with MTConnect and MT*Insight* certainly being on that prestigious list. I would not want to be the person who follows in Doug's shoes at AMT.

If you have not done so already, go check out MTInsight.org today!

217

[MC]² MTConnect: Connecting Manufacturing Conference Thanks

Sincere and special thanks to my close friends Chris Melissinos, Mike Geldner, John Meyer, and Steve Fritzinger.

- Chris gave a keynote at [MC]² 2011 titled, "Anytime, Anywhere Manufacturing in the 21st Century."

- Mike gave a keynote at [MC]² 2011 titled, "Inside The World of Google."

- Steve gave a keynote at [MC]² 2013 titled, "Manufacturing with Darwin, Moore and Metcalfe."

- John gave a keynote at [MC]² 2013 titled, "Processing Zetabytes: The Technologies Enabling Big Data and Analytics."

As The Beatles once wrote, "I get by with a little help from my friends." Well, when I made the suggestion for a MTConnect Conference and then was given the reins by Paul Warndorf and Doug Woods (as well as MTConnect's Board of Directors) to make it happen, I had a serious problem to deal with. That problem was I needed *great* speakers who were technical gods and *fantastic* in front of large audiences. Do you know how many people fall into that category? Slim and none, and Slim just left town. Chris, Mike, Steve, and John all gave incredible keynotes at the [MC]². I am very, very lucky to have such smart, innovative, passionate, and great friends. Huge congratulations to Chris who received the Ambassador Award at the Game Developers Conference 2013 (GDC13) in San Francisco the week of March 25–29 for his amazing work curating "The Art of Video Games," an exhibition at the Smithsonian American Art Museum in 2012.

AMT's Exhibitions, Communications, and Meetings Departments are all the envy of the entire manufacturing world and are on a whole new level compared to everyone else at any other company. OK, I am biased, but I know it is true.

Chris Rasul, VP of meetings at AMT, and her team seem to pull off miracles at every conference AMT runs. This is true of [MC]² as well. Chris has Beth Czupil and Leti Marquez on her team. Beth really ran [MC]² 2011, and she did an amazing job. She did an equally outstanding job with [MC]² 2013. Plus, Beth has the best sense of humor at AMT, which says a lot. Leti ran the exhibits for [MC]² 2013, and it was a real success.

Bonnie Gurney's leadership with communications is second to none in the industry. I have lost track of all the great suggestions and guidance that Bonnie has given me over the years. Penny Brown is the ultimate editor. She is extremely creative and very fast in her writing abilities. Penny wears many hats at AMT, including being in front of the camera, a very creative writer as well as editor and she excels at all of them. Penny has helped me out over the years with IMTS Insider articles, articles I wrote for magazines, video content, advertisements, [MC]², and this does not include the countless projects that she has created and led for a number of MTConnect and MT*Insight* opportunities. Penny also captures lots of great content by interviewing speakers and attendees at the [MC]²s over the years. Moni Haley is one of the world's best graphics designers. Moni's creativity is unparalleled and her follow-through on projects is flawless. If Moni says she is going to get something done by a given date, you can take it to the bank and absolutely know it will be first class, on time, and on budget. She does this and instead of sleeping at night like the rest of us, she works at a fire department. Moni is truly an amazing individual. Thanks to Pam Kachel for all of her great help with [MC]² conferences. Pam has really helped [MC]² in so many ways.

Thanks to Linda Montfort, VP of finance and HR for AMT, and her entire staff for all their help with the [MC]² conferences. Specifically thanks to Lillie Santiago, Helen Nguyen, and Linda Syrek. Thanks to Bill Herman for the great ideas he shared with me on improving [MC]². Thanks to John Krisko for his guidance with MTConnect at IMTS. Thanks to Greg Jones for his work on Smartforce Development as this helped my thinking in putting together some of the labs for [MC]² 2013. Thanks to Amber Thomas for her great insight into how the government works because this really helped in many ways in our MTConnect efforts in working with government folks at [MC]² and on committees as well.

Thanks to Adam Baker, Austin Burns, and Pee Wee Pearson for all their help with the [MC]² conferences over the years. Adam, Austin, and Pee Wee did a lot of the work that really helped drive attendance up at both [MC]² 2011 and [MC]² 2013.

Special Thanks

Sheila Kaplan is the person who keeps everything together when it comes to MTConnect and [MC]². Sheila works for Paul Warndorf, and if there is a better executive administrator than Sheila Kaplan, I surely have not met nor heard of that person. Sheila seems to have a photographic memory and is the most organized person I have ever met. She has perfect follow through. Sheila is retiring in July of 2013. She can't be replaced, as that would be impossible. Thanks Sheila for all your help and guidance over the years!

A huge thanks to Lois Uthman, director of IT for AMT, and her staff, which is the best IT staff on planet Earth. These brilliant and passionate individuals include: Asim Mukhtar, Heather Richwine, Laura Furman, and Myrta Mason.

Sincere thanks to Laurie Stone for her many suggestions on how to write a book and how to avoid the many potholes along the way. Special thanks as well to both Sue Walls of Walls Lithographics and Suzanne Leonard of Word Style, LLC. I had the privilege of working for Sue while at Sun Microsystems, and Sue is second to none in her leadership abilities. I am also very fortunate to call her a friend. Sue and her son Marty are the ones who really helped me with this book and published it. Sue also introduced me to my editor.

Suzanne did a fantastic job editing this book, creating great graphics as well as providing me with countless great suggestions on how to make it flow and read better. Suzanne is a true professional, and I am very fortunate that Sue recommended her to me. This was my first book and I sincerely appreciate all of Suzanne's patience with my beginner questions, as well as the countless changes that I kept sending at her. I learned a ton from Suzanne it made my life much easier because I was in the hands of an absolute professional with many years of experience. Suzanne made countless suggestions that I never would have thought of and it made my book much, much better. I strongly recommend Suzanne Leonard and her company Word Style, LLC for anyone who is looking for a GREAT editor!

The Final Word

When I was at Sun Microsystems, I gave numerous talks to colleges and universities. Typically, the talks were held in the Engineering Department or the Computer Science Department. Usually, the audience would be mostly students with a few professors attending. The talks were always technical, but I would end my talk with a slide that would give them some basic financial and life advice.

The first was basic financial advice, and I call this Dave Edstrom's RELY for them to remember how to think about finances:

- **Retirement.** Compound interest is a magical formula. Go read the book by David Chilton called, *The Wealthy Barber* to understand finances and how to think about money and how to save.

221

- **Emergency Funds.** Not if, but when emergencies happen

- **Living Expenses.** Do the math.

- **You.** Finally have fun. As author Jerry Hopkins wrote in in the biography of the late Jim Morrison of The Doors—*No One Gets Out of Here Alive.*

I would also tell them Dave Edstrom's Law of Eternal Happiness, which is, "Never, *EVER* sleep with someone who has more problems than you do!" I would then add, "and you can practice that tonight." Always leave 'em laughing has been my motto in public speaking and in life.

The last advice I would give would be on life. I would tell them that I want them to remember three things:

- Life is short.
- Death is certain.
- If you don't make your own decisions now, time will make them for you.

It was the third point on making your own decisions that I would emphasize with the students. This applies in life and it applies in business. Do not wait to apply the lessons in this book on how to think about technology and do not wait to investigate MTConnect, do it *now*!

I really hope you enjoyed reading this book. Any suggestions, please drop me a note.

Finally, and most importantly, thanks again to my best friend in the world, the love of my life, who also happens to be my wife—Julie Hall Johnson Edstrom.

Glossary

(From MTConnect Standard, Unless Otherwise Noted)

Adapter
: An optional software component that connects the Agent to the Device.

Agent
: A process that implements the MTConnect® HTTP protocol, XML generation, and MTConnect protocol.

Alarm
: An alarm indicates an event that requires attention and indicates a deviation from normal operation. Alarms are reported in MTConnect as Condition.

Application
: A process or set of processes that access the MTConnect® Agent to perform some task.

Attribute
: A part of an XML element that provides additional information about that XML element. For example, the name XML element of the Device is given as <Device name="mill-1">...</Device>

CDATA
: The text in a simple content element. For example, This is some text, in <Message ...>This is some text</Message>.

Component
: A part of a device that can have sub-components and data items. A component is a basic building block of a device.

Controlled Vocabulary
: The value of an element or attribute is limited to a restricted set of

possibilities. Examples of controlled vocabularies are country codes: US, JP, CA, FR, DE, etc....

Current
: A snapshot request to the Agent to retrieve the current values of all the data items specified in the path parameter. If no path parameter is given, then the values for all components are provided.

Data Item
: A data item provides the descriptive information regarding something that can be collected by the Agent.

Device
: A piece of equipment capable of performing an operation. A device may be composed of a set of components that provide data to the application. The device is a separate entity with at least one component or data item providing information about the device.

Discovery
: Discovery is a service that allows the application to locate Agents for devices in the manufacturing environment. The discovery service is also referred to as the Name Service.

DNS
: The Domain Name System (DNS) is a hierarchical distributed naming system for computers, services, or any resource connected to the Internet or a private network. It associates various information with domain names assigned to each of the participating entities. Most prominently, it translates domain names meaningful for users to

the numerical IP addresses needed for the purpose of locating computer services and devices worldwide. By providing a worldwide, distributed keyword-based redirection service, the Domain Name System is an essential component of the functionality of the Internet.

An often-used analogy to explain the Domain Name System is that it serves as the phone book for the Internet by translating human-friendly computer hostnames into IP addresses. For example, the domain name www.example.com translates to the addresses 192.0.43.10 (IPv4) and 2620:0:2d0:200::10 (IPv6). Unlike a phone book, the DNS can be quickly updated, allowing a service's location on the network to change without affecting the end users, who continue to use the same host name. Users take advantage of this when they recite meaningful Uniform Resource Locators (URLs) and e-mail addresses without having to know how the computer actually locates the services. NOTE: This definition is from Wikipedia.

OOP

Object Oriented Programming is a programming paradigm that represents concepts as "objects" that have data fields (attributes that describe the object) and associated procedures known as methods. Objects, which are usually instances of classes, are used to interact with one another to design applications and computer programs. NOTE: This definition is from Wikipedia.

Event
An event represents a change in state that occurs at a point in time. Note: An event does not occur at predefined frequencies.

HTTP
Hyper-Text Transport Protocol. The protocol used by all web browsers and web applications.

Instance
When used in software engineering, the word instance is used to define a single physical example of that type. In object-oriented models, there is the class that describes the thing and the instance that is an example of that thing.

Java
Java is a general-purpose, concurrent, class-based, object-oriented computer programming language that is specifically designed to have as few implementation dependencies as possible. It is intended to let application developers "write once, run anywhere" (WORA), meaning that code that runs on one platform does not need to be recompiled to run on another. Java applications are typically compiled to bytecode (class file) that can run on any Java virtual machine (JVM) regardless of computer architecture. Java is, as of 2012, one of the most popular programming languages in use, particularly for client-server web

applications, with a reported 10 million users.[10][11] Java was originally developed by James Gosling at Sun Microsystems (which has since merged into Oracle Corporation) and released in 1995 as a core component of Sun Microsystems' Java platform. The language derives much of its syntax from C and C++, but it has fewer low-level facilities than either of them. NOTE: This definition is from Wikipedia.

LDAP   Lightweight Directory Access Protocol, better known as Active Directory in Microsoft Windows. This protocol provides resource location and contact information in a hierarchal structure.

MIME   Multipurpose Internet Mail Extensions. A format used for encoding multipart mail and http content with separate sections separated by a fixed boundary.

Probe   A request to determine the configuration and reporting capabilities of the device.

REST   REpresentational State Transfer. A software architecture where the client and server move through a series of state transitions based solely on the request from the client and the response from the server.

Results   A general term for the Samples, Events, and Condition contained in a ComponentStream as a response from a sample or current request.

Sample	A sample is a data point from within a continuous series of data points. An example of a Sample is the position of an axis.
Socket	When used concerning inter-process communication, it refers to a connection between two end-points (usually processes). Socket communication most often uses TCP/IP as the underlying protocol.
Stream	A collection of Events, Samples, and Condition organized by devices and components.
Service	An application that provides necessary functionality.
Tag	Used to reference an instance of an XML element.
TCP/IP	The Internet protocol suite is the set of communications protocols used for the Internet and similar networks, and generally the most popular protocol stack for wide area networks. It is commonly known as TCP/IP, because of its most important protocols: Transmission Control Protocol (TCP) and Internet Protocol (IP), which were the first networking protocols defined in this standard. It is occasionally known as the DoD model due to the foundational influence of the ARPANET in the 1970s (operated by DARPA, an agency of the United States Department

of Defense). NOTE: This definition is from Wikipedia.

URI   A uniform resource identifier (URI) is a string of characters used to identify a name or a resource. Such identification enables interaction with representations of the resource over a network (typically the World Wide Web) using specific protocols. Schemes specifying a concrete syntax and associated protocols define each URI. URIs can be classified as locators (URLs), as names (URNs), or as both. A uniform resource name (URN) functions like a person's name, while a uniform resource locator (URL) resembles that person's street address. In other words: the URN defines an item's identity, while the URL provides a method for finding it. NOTE: This definition is from Wikipedia.

URL   A uniform resource locator, abbreviated URL, also known as web address, is a specific character string that constitutes a reference to a resource. In most web browsers, the URL of a web page is displayed on top inside an address bar. NOTE: This definition is from Wikipedia.

URN   A Uniform Resource Name (URN) is the historical name for a Uniform Resource Identifier (URI) that uses the urn: scheme.

Defined in 1997 in RFC 2141, URNs were intended to serve as persistent, location-independent identifiers for resources, allowing the simple mapping of namespaces into a single URN namespace.[1] The existence of such a URI does not imply availability of the identified resource, but such URIs are required to remain globally unique and persistent even when the resource ceases to exist or becomes unavailable.[2] NOTE: This definition is from Wikipedia

UUID
Universally unique identifier.

XPath
XPath is a language for addressing parts of an XML Document. See the XPath specification for more information. http://www.w3.org/TR/xpath

XML
Extensible Markup Language. http://www.w3.org/XML/

XML Schema
The definition of the XML structure and vocabularies used in the XML Document.

XML Document
An instance of an XML Schema, which has a single, root XML element and conforms to the XML specification and schema.

XML Element
An element is the central building block of any XML Document. For example, in MTConnect® the Device XML element is specified as <Device >...</Device>

XML NMTOKEN
The data type for XML identifiers. It MUST start with a letter, an underscore "_" or a colon ":" and then it MUST be

followed by a letter, a number, or one of the following ".", "-", "_", ":". An NMTOKEN cannot have any spaces or special characters.

About the Author

Dave Edstrom is the CEO/CTO for Virtual Photons Electrons, president and chairman of the board for the MTConnect Institute and has been in the computer industry for more than 34 years. Dave worked for Sun Microsystems for almost 23 years in a variety of leadership positions. Dave has held a variety of positions ranging from an assembler programmer, technical management, system engineer, chief technologist, technical director, and principal engineer for a variety of companies. Dave has been working with Unix since 1981. From 1987 to 2010 Dave was with Sun Microsystems in a variety of technical leadership roles. Dave was the Chief Technologist for the Sun Microsystems Software Practice from 2004 through 2010.

Dave has been a key contributor to the MTConnect standard from its inception. Dave, along with Dr. David Patterson of University of California at Berkeley, planted the seed and laid the foundation for MTConnect at the 2006 Association for Manufacturing Technology's (AMT) Annual Meeting at Lake Las Vegas, Nevada.

Dave has had the privilege of working with Paul Warndorf, VP of technology for AMT, who is the true leader of MTConnect; Will Sobel, president of System Insights and the chief architect of MTConnect; John Turner, director of Technology for FA Consulting and Technology (FAC&T), who is the shepherd for the MTConnect Standard; John Byrd, president of AMT during the initial years of MTConnect and a thought leader in manufacturing; and most importantly, Doug Woods, president of AMT, who is a true visionary who is redefining manufacturing and was the chairman of the board at AMT at the beginning of MTConnect and now as president of

AMT continues to personally drive MTConnect to be a reality. There are many others, but it is important to point out those five.

Since early in 2010, Dave has been working as a consultant for AMT as the director for the Office of Strategic Innovation working primarily in two areas—MTConnect and MT*Insight.* Dave was named president and chairman of the board for the MTConnect Institute in May 2010 and continues in that role today. When Dave is not working on technology for his company Virtual Photons Electrons, or doing consulting at AMT working on MTConnect or MT*Insight,* or consulting for other companies, he enjoys his one wife, his three sons, his two dogs, and his two Corvettes.

If you have any comments or suggestions on how this book could be improved, please send them me at: DavidAllenEdstrom@gmail.com.

The reader can also go to http://ToMeasureIsToKnow.com for updates.

Index

Endnotes

1 Surowiecki, James. "Turn of the Century." Wired Jan. 2002. Print.

2 Scharf, Thomas J., and Thompson Westcott, History of Philadelphia. 1609-1884. Phil. L.H. Everts and Co., 1884.

3 Gilbert, K. R., & Galloway, D. F., 1978, "Machine Tools." In C. Singer, et al., (Eds.), A history of technology. Oxford, Clarendon Press & Lee, S. (Ed.), 1900, Dictionary of national biography, Vol LXI. Smith Elder, London

4 Gilbert

5 McCabe, Brian. National Public Radio (NPR). "The Friday Podcast: Buttons And Other Connectors." NPR.org Planet Money. NPR: Oct. 8, 2010. Web.

6 Brooks, Frederick P. The Mythical Man-Month: Essays on Software Engineering. Reading, Mass. Addison-Wesley, 2012. Print.

7 Lehrer, Jonah. Imagine: How Creativity Works. Boston: Houghton Mifflin Harcourt, 2012. Print.

8 Hancock, LynNell. "Why Are Finland's Schools Successful?" Smithsonian Sept. 2011. Print.

9 Telander, Rick. *Heaven Is a Playground.* U of Nebraska Press, 2004.

10 Gladwell, Malcolm. Outliers: Why Some People Succeed and Some Don't. New York: Little Brown & Co, 2008. Print.

11 "Make (magazine)." Wikipedia. March 23, 2013. http://en.wikipedia.org/wiki/Make_(magazine)

Wikipedia creative commons attribution license: http://en.wikipedia.org/wiki/Wikipedia:Text_of_Creative_Commons_Attribu tion-ShareAlike_3.0_Unported_License

12 Darwin, Charles, and George L. Levine. *The Origin of Species by Means of Natural Selection.* New York: Barnes & Noble Classics, 2004. Print.

13 Armbrust, Michael; Armando Fox; Rean Griffith; Anthony D. Joseph; Randy Katz; Andy Konwinski; Gunho Lee; David Patterson; Ariel Rabkin; Ion Stoica; and Matei Zaharia. "Above the Clouds: A View of Cloud Computing." UC Berkeley Reliable Adaptive Distributed systems Laboratory (RAD Lab).

14 Kliff, Sarah. "Study: Most Radiologists Don't Notice a Gorilla in a CT Scan." The Washington Post. Feb. 19, 2013.

15 "Inattentional blindness." Wikipedia. Feb. 28, 2013. http://en.wikipedia.org/wiki/Inattentional_blindness

16 Schefter, James L. *All Corvettes Are Red: The Rebirth of an American Legend.* New York: Simon & Schuster, 1997. Print.

17 "Smart grid." Wikipedia. Feb. 5, 2013. http://en.wikipedia.org/wiki/Smart_grid

[18] "Across the U.S. Utilities Share Experiences from Smart Grid Deployments." SmartGrid.gov. www.smartgrid.gov/federal_initiatives/featured_initiatives/across_us_utilities_share_experiences_smart_grid_deployments. March 20, 2013.

[19] Chiappinelli, Chris. "A Sneak Peak Into Manufacturing's Future." Manufacturing Executive. February 22, 2013. http://www.manufacturing-executive.com/message/3753

[20] "Business Intelligence." Wikipedia. http://en.wikipedia.org/wiki/Business_intelligence. March 20, 2013.

[21] Albert, Mark. "Manufacturing Game-Changer, MTConnect." Modern Machine Shop Dec 2009. Print.

[22] Sweatt, A.J. "MTConnect Adds Great Value, Potential." http://ajsweatt.com/mtconnect-adds-great-value-potential/ January 5, 2013.

[23] "Curtiss Wright Controls." Case Studies. MTConnect Institute. http://mtconnect.org/overview/mtconnect-overview/case-studies.aspx.March 20, 2013.

[24] "Getting Started with MTConnect: Connectivity Guide." MTConnect.org. http://mtconnect.org/media/7312/getting_started_with_mtconnect_-_final.pdf. March 20, 2013

[25] "MTConnect® and [MC]2: a bright future ahead." AMT News. AMTonline. http://www.amtonline.org/newsroom/AMTNEWS/mtconnectandmc2abrightfutureahead.htm

[26] Gladwell, Malcolm. Featured Book Review: *Outliers*. Concordville, Pa: Soundview Executive Book Summaries, 2009. Internet resource.

[27] Donahue, Deirdre. "Malcolm Gladwell's 'Success' defines 'outlier' achievement." *USA Today*. http://usatoday30.usatoday.com/life/books/news/2008-11-17-gladwell-success_N.htm

[28] Coyle, Daniel. *The Talent Code: Greatness Isn't Born: It's Grown, Here's How*. New York: Bantam Books, 2009. Print.

Made in the USA
San Bernardino, CA
17 July 2013